tell you what those dangers of visibility are. Beyond the issue of safety, visibility is reducing their being to a single identity - stealing them of their humanity and excluding them from the rest of society.

The visual, in the art world, as well as in social media (both of which are controlled by capitalist forces) is also linked, in different ways, to enforcement of particular aesthetic regimes, to body facism, to the monetization of information and to exploitation and profit.

The works presented in this exhibition present two different approaches to the issue of visibility; one that uses visibility to make one's identity visible, to amplify voices and as a tool of protest. Other works, sometimes even for the same ends, use masquerade, concealment and defacement or do away entirely with the visual and use audio and texts. These works highlight social and political issues and yet others question the politics of visibility itself.

The works point to the fact that the Other is more than what is visible. They use invisibility as an invitation, as a space where the viewer can dwell. As an act of radical hospitality, they create a place without designation (identity) for an unknown guest who is yet

to come. Following Levinas, it can be said that in these works where "the totality breaks up" the viewer can find "the gleam of exteriority or transcendence in the fade of the other" I believe that some of the works in "The Face of the Other" trace such spaces, and others - constituting it - offer the viewer a more ethical vision and a less violent ways of seeing .

Gil Mualem-Doron,
SEAS Creative Director,
Exhibition Curator.

I0390814

SEAS (Socially Engaged Art Salon) champions socially engaged art, promotes artists from underrepresented communities, and is committed to equality, diversity, and inclusion in the art sector. SEAS operates at the Black and Ethnic Minorities Community Partnership (BMECP) Centre and at the LGBTQAI+ Ledward Centre.

Recent projects:
Watermarks (2021),
Estuary 2021; "*Where are we?*" (2020),
FrancisKnight; *somewhere* (2020),
SEAS/Brighton Festival; edge/threshold/
brink (2018) Nuit Blanche
Toronto.

Maria is currently a PhD candidate at the Royal College of Art, London.

MARIA

AMIDU

@ms_amidu
www.mariaand.co
www.thewhereing.com/episodes/episode02/mariaamidu/thisunbelongingbelongstome

6

CONTENTS

6 Maria Amidu

16 Josef Cabey

26 L'Enfant

32 Nelson Morales

40 Mengwen Cao

48 Arit Etukudo

52 Tugba Tirpan

60 Jenny Nash

66 Gil Mualem Doron

74 Ryan Peter French

78 Beth Easton

82 K-Pup

88 Constanza Miranda

94 Aubane Berthomé Martínez

98 Charlie Wood

102 Sisters Uncut

The Face Of The Other

"Welcoming guests is greater than receiving the Divine Presence"
(The Talmud, Shabbat 127a:13)

"Share with God's people who are in need. Practice hospitality." (Romans 12:13 NIV)

"He who believes in Allah and the Last Day should show hospitality to his guest" (Sahih Muslim hadith, Book 1 Hadith 75)

"whether it be the foreigner in general, the immigrant, the exiled, the deported, the stateless or the displaced person ... we would ask these new cities of refuge to reorient the politics of the state." (Derrida, J. On Cosmopolitanism and Forgiveness, London and New York: Routledge, 2001).

This exhibition starts with an invitation - an invitation to face an Other without seeing. To welcome an Other without knowing. Because the face of the Other always hides. It is a mask that conceals the irreducible difference or Otherness. This mask,

with neither an invitation nor with intention, shelters us from infinite alterity. As such, the face of the Other is invariably related to hospitality and to inclusion that in fact derives from radical Otherness.

In libral democracies, visibility, representation and inclusion stand together. Making something or someone(s) visible is an important act in political and social struggles, especially for LGBTQ communities. Visibility is directly linked to representation and political power and to the right to protest. In the arts context, making something/someone visible is one of the most important strategies or consequences of socially and politically engaged art and of relational aesthetics.

However, visibility, especially when enforced, is associated with systems of colonisation, of surveillance and control. For various groups such as refugees, transgender people, homeless people, people of colour and religious minorities, visibility is always also a risk. Ask any black or brown kid who was stopped and searched, any visibly disabled person, any homeless person, any migrant who does not look like a local, a veiled Muslim woman, any trans preson who cannot "pass" or any queer looking person - they will

SOMEWHERE

"Somewhere is a collection of one-minute, experimental films. The work evolved from 'A seat at the table – a meal and conversation at SEAS between a group of artists in January 2020. somewhere was originally planned as part of a physical exhibition during Brighton Festival 2020 but due to the Covid-19 restrictions, the work became digital.

Following the meal, Maria wrote a series of texts taking the participating artists' original words as a starting point and later invited the artists to recite the transformed words for the films.

Somewhere is a testament to stories told during 'A seat at the table' and speaks to the troublesome, contingent and precarious nature of being seen to be from elsewhere."

Contributing artists included:

Ainoa Burgos Gonzalez /Gil Mualem Doron / Edi Jay Mandala / Estabrak / Hong Dam / Maria Amidu / Tugba Tirpan

Maria Amidu is a UK-based visual artist and writer, developing national and international site-specific and public realm projects. Her artistic concerns are influenced by the scope and significance of common experiences. She is interested in the relationships between people and place and what is hidden, obscured or unspoken in various social situations, using these elements as a means to try and substantiate myriad lived experiences.

so what do you say to someone who comes from elsewhere, how do you make sense of the place you are in, distinguish between the cacophony and the reality, the tangible situation, the noises that send you in the wrong direction; interruption, misinformation, constant movement, constant change; point me to a place, the place that is quiet, less faces, less chatter, more meaningful conversation; picture postcards and drawings of somewhere, dark marks on a foldout page saying you are here to some and stay the fuck away from me to others; over there, stand over there, stay back, don't touch me and don't touch my stuff: how do you navigate this rejection, how do we fortify ourselves in this mess

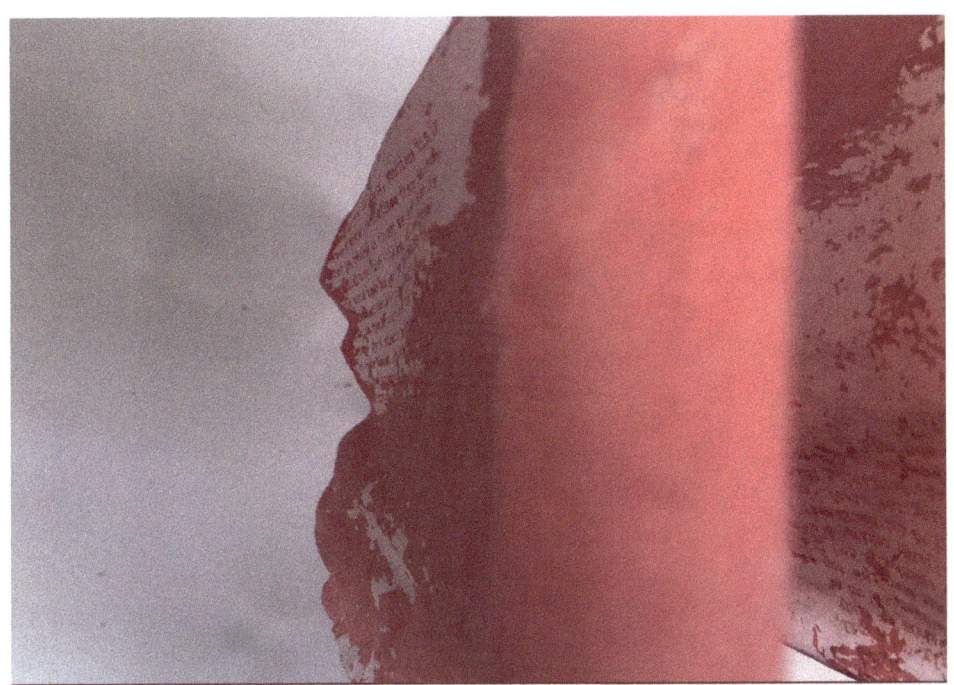

the causes attached to leaving and returning, sometimes this is freedom of movement and sometimes there is force; what gets retained are voices; we catch these in out mind's eye and we hold them close, replaying the words again and again; how do we resolve these disconnects, how do the spaces we recall speak to us, do the walls remember, is that how we define home by the whispers we feel when we press our ears to the flat surface, letting it brush the recollections across our cheeks, is this what we must carry to get a purchase on the in-between, our rememberings holding it all in place

craving
this happens to me when I am lonely or unwell,
trying to imagine the flavours i know my body
remembers, stumbling through the recreation of
meals I named in another language when the top of
my head was parallel with the countertop and I'd
do a child-type version of helping, making a mess
and possibly causing frustration and amusement and
unnecessary tlearing up; tasting the sweetness of
this and the saltiness of that, comparing this
sensory delight with the silence when the pots becam
became empty and the stove was cold to the touch

this happens to me when i am lonely or unwell, trying to
imagine the flavours i know my body remembers, stumbling
through the recreation of meals i named in another language
when the top of my head was parallel with the countertop
and i'd do a child-type version of helping, making a mess and
possibly causing frustration and amusement and unnecessary
clearing up; tasting the sweetness of this and the saltiness of
that, comparing this sensory delight with the silence and
stillness when the pots became empty and the stove was
cold to touch

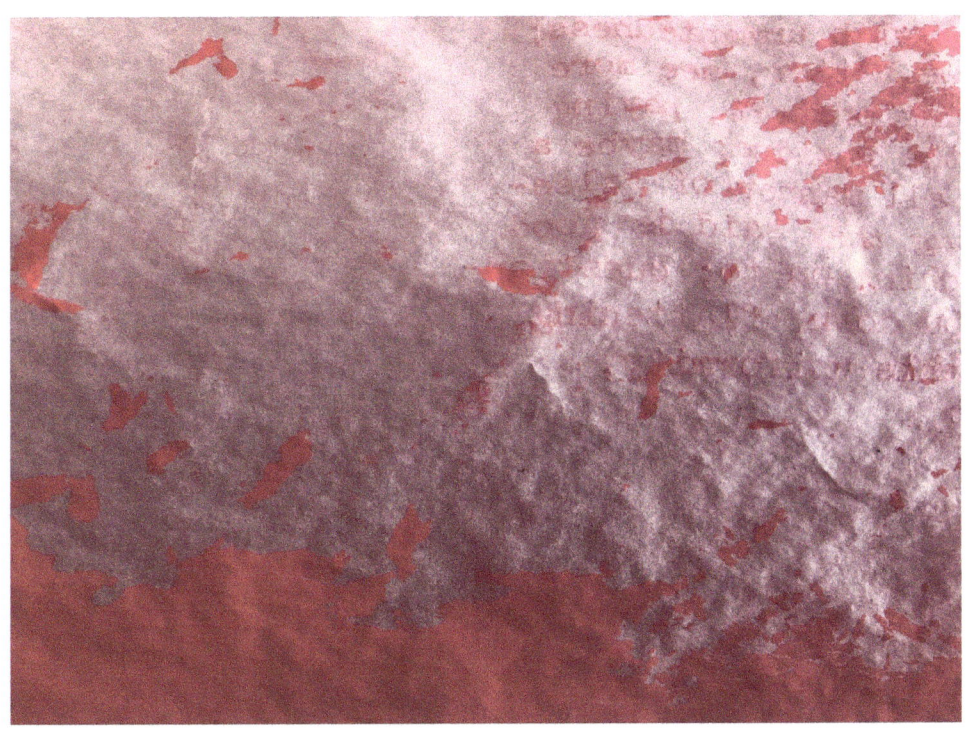

something that falls, is out of balance, that trickles away, something administered to alleviate the pain, something landing and making a splash, marking the surface with unwantedness; ointment for the eyes to see better, see more clearly what exactly is going on here, paying attention to the detail, the residue; maybe a barrier to protect against all manner of falsehood wrapped up as something they said is good for you; letting go of, catching on to; questioning, weightedness holding you down, flattening everything to an unrecognisable uniformity, making us guarded and alert

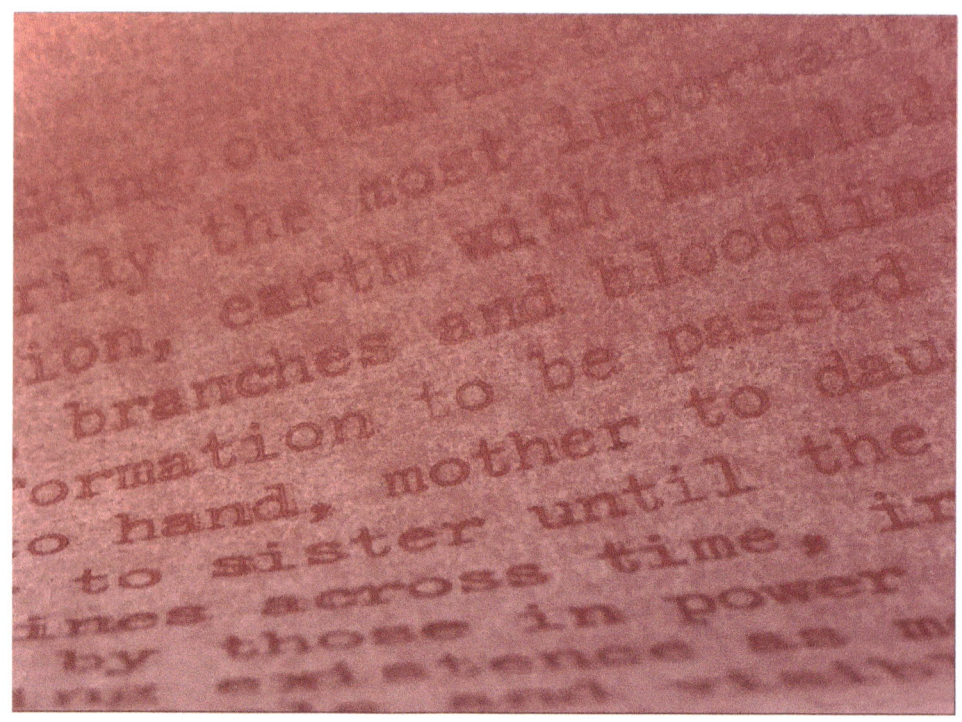

trees stretching outwards towards the oldest but not necessarily the most important, landscapes which question, earth with knowledge that cannot be ignored, branches and bloodlines forming a mesh of information to be passed back and forth from hand to hand, mother to daughter, father to son, sister to sister until the heritage becomes indelible lines across time, irrefutable and uncontested by those in power and those on the street, seeing existence as more than survival, as something whole and visible and solid to the touch, viewpoints on a horizon with equal breathing space

that sentence three times over and over insisting to be answered; creating a shape with the added elements that work for them regardless of what you just actually said, beach paraphernalia to hide behind, face forward gazing at the clear blue water instead of at the lives you know are pressing on the back of your neck, the heat making everything brittle and fragile to the touch, the pieces collected and reassembled to show a different and more important narrative, one where the swearwords have not been cut out and tucked under the wet sand where the land meets sea; using your voice to explain and explain and explain

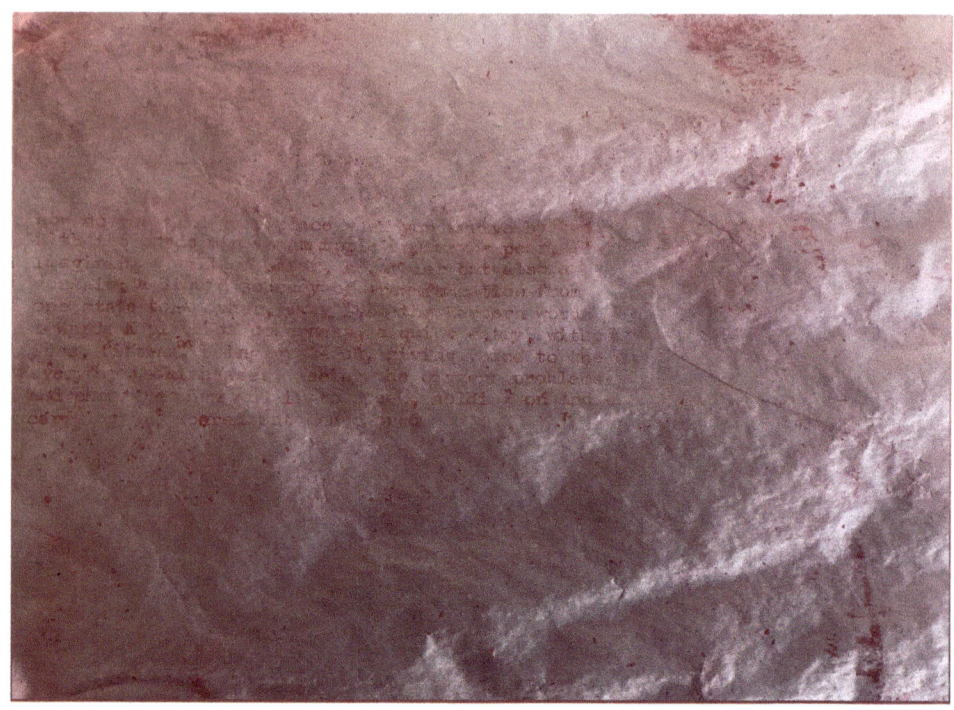

how do you find your place when you arrived by boat with only the words man, woman, apple and maybe pear; I'm imagining a wall of water, a barrier but also a curtain, a liquid journey of transformation from one state to another, away from Eastern words towards a place of otherness; a quiet entry, giving voice to everyday unfairnesses, recognising the bigger problems and choosing when and if to speak, holding on and carrying on, moored but unanchored

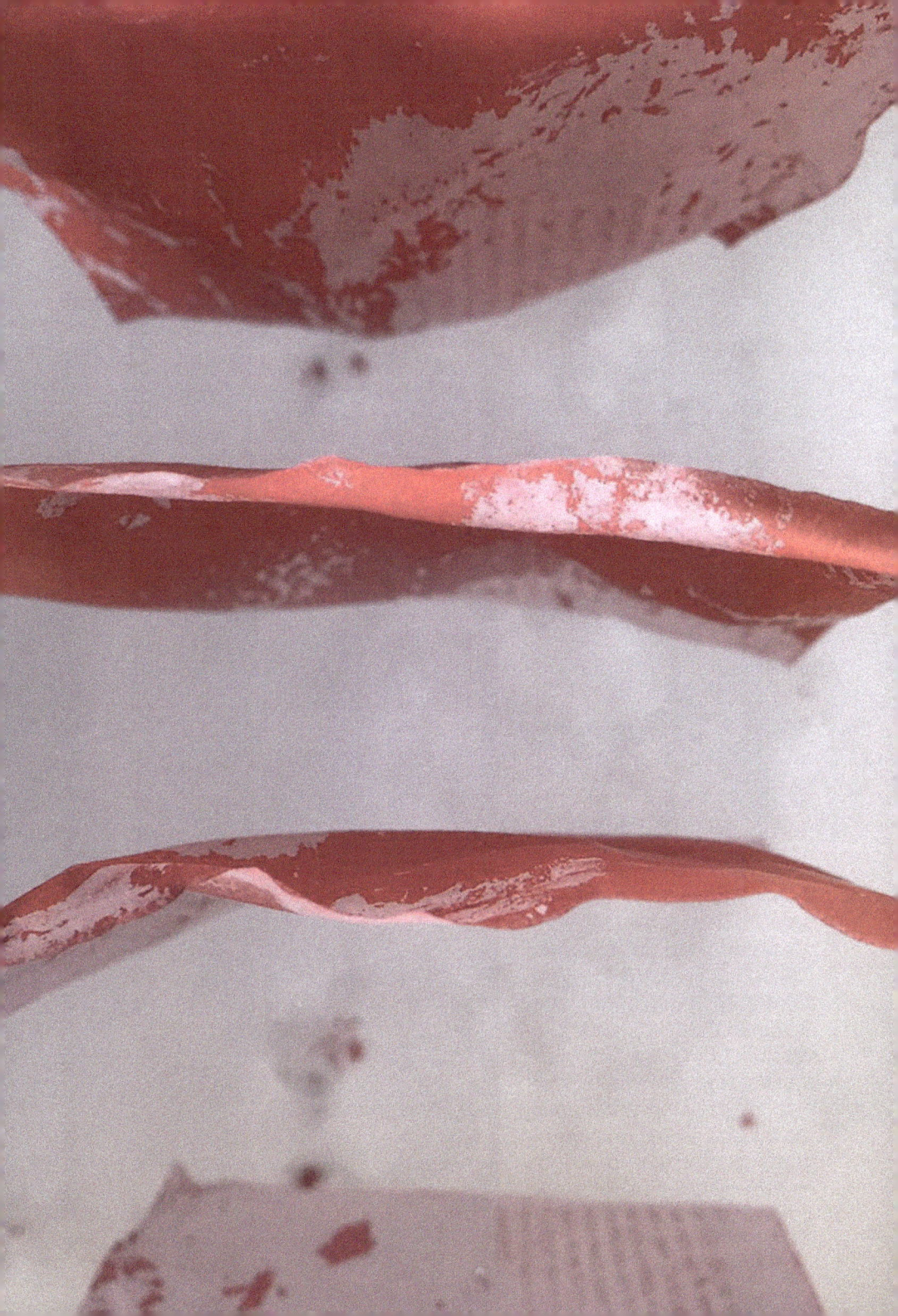

JOSEF CABEY

Born in London, Josef relocated to Brighton in 2003. He was educated at Newham College (Dip, Art & Design), Central St Martins (BA Hons, Graphic Design), and University of Brighton (MA information studies) where he is also a part time librarian in the college of Arts & Humanities. Josef has also practiced as a freelance illustrator and graphic designer.

Looking at you

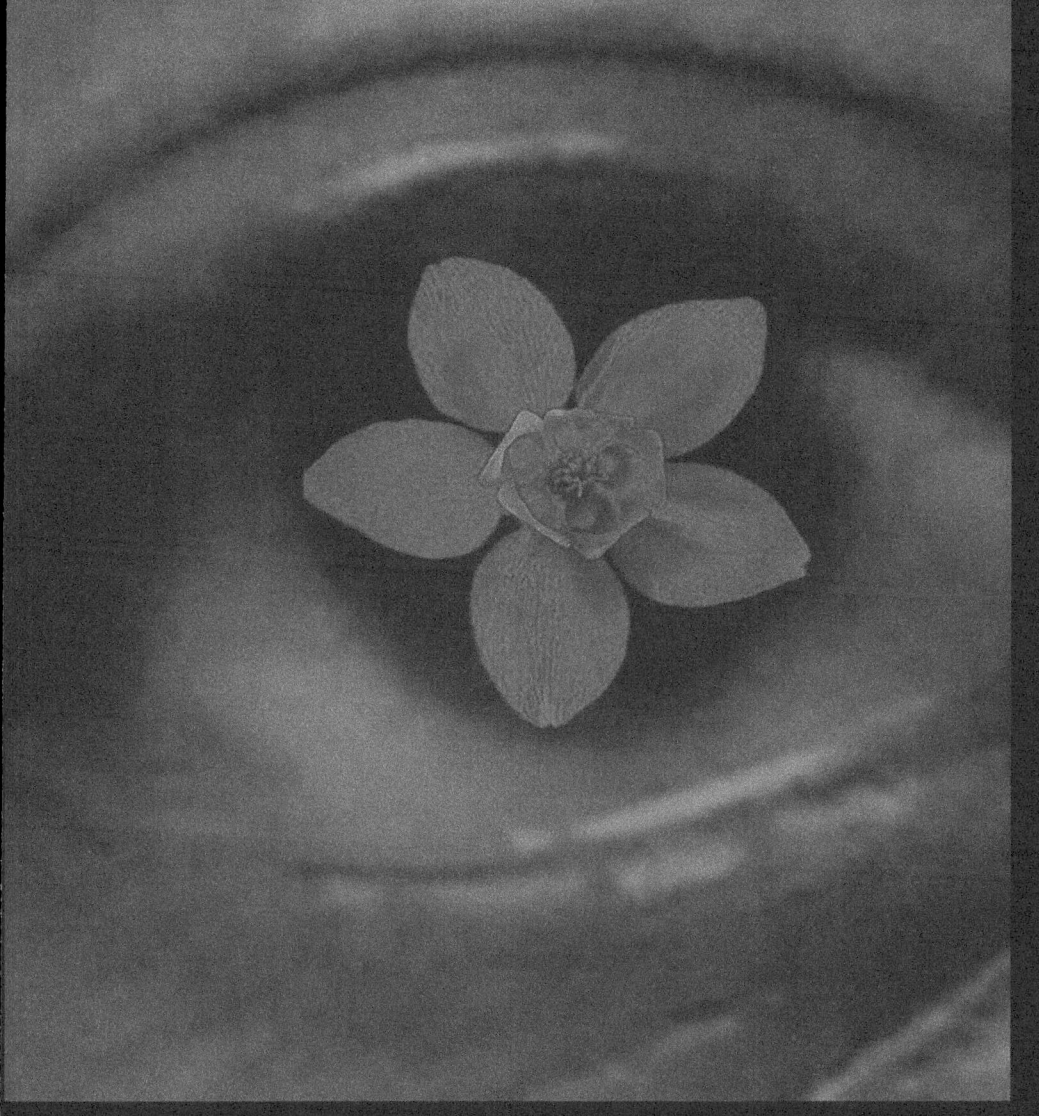

Looking at me

The witness said: A profiling box

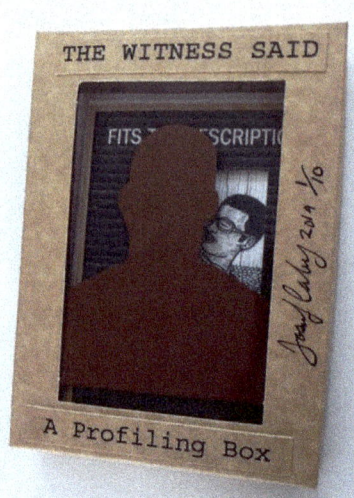
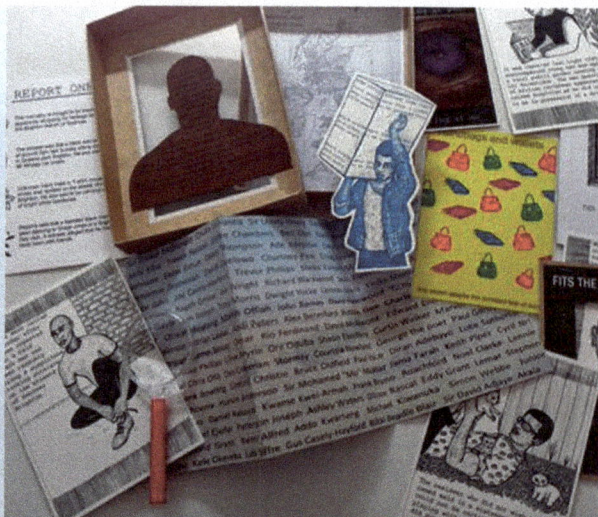

'The witness said' is an artist's box (limited edition of 10) based on my recent series of paintings that investigate instances of racial profiling of black men in the UK. The original paintings were first shown in Eastbourne, Worthing, Hastings and Brighton as part of the Constructed Geographies exhibition in 2018/19. Some of the work is based on personal experiences living in Brighton & Hove and highlights the sometimes absurd instances in which racial profiling sometimes occurs. There are 12 key elements in the box that can be engaged with in a manner of your own choosing to engage and reflect upon the subject depicted.

www.josefcabeyart.com

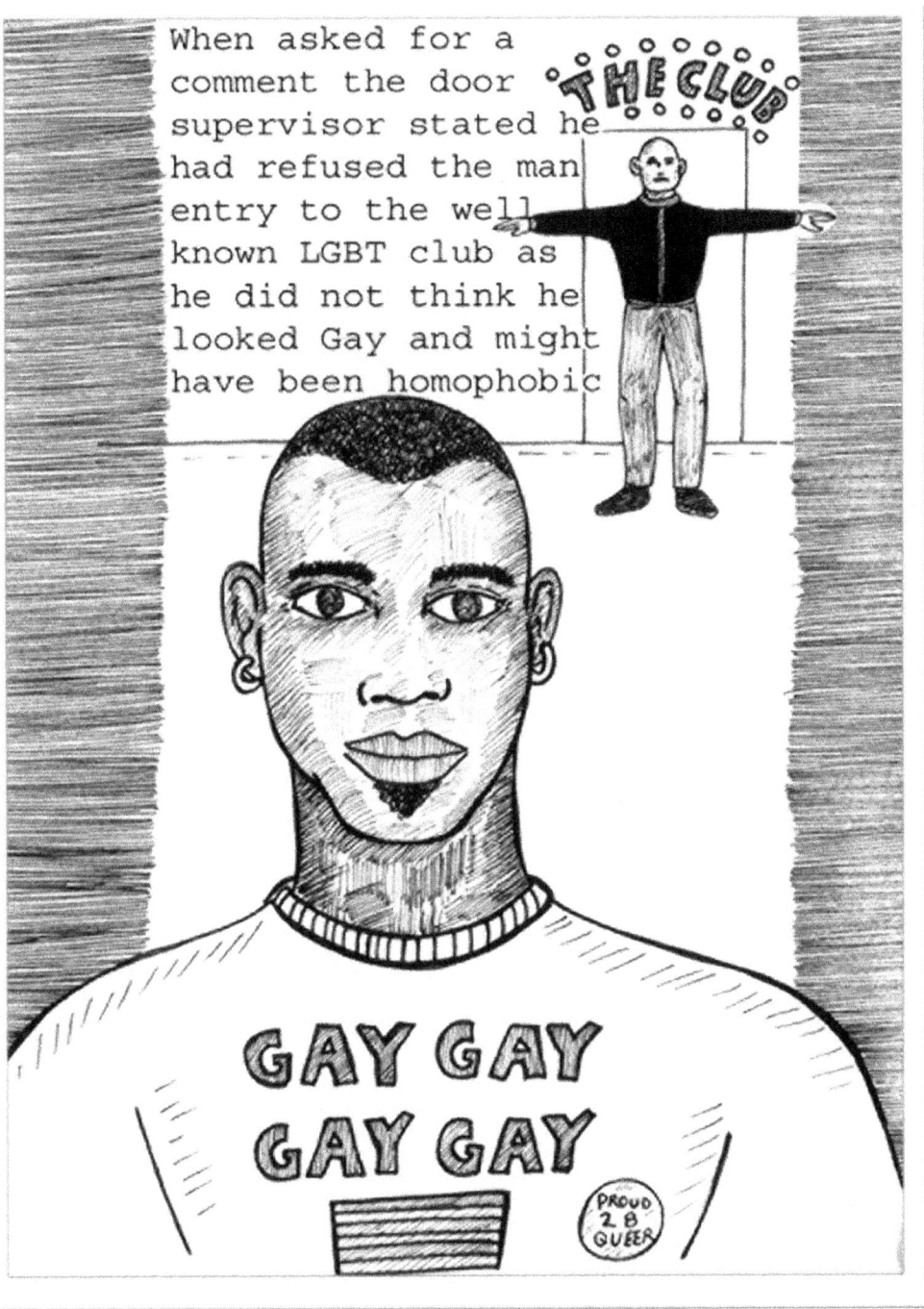

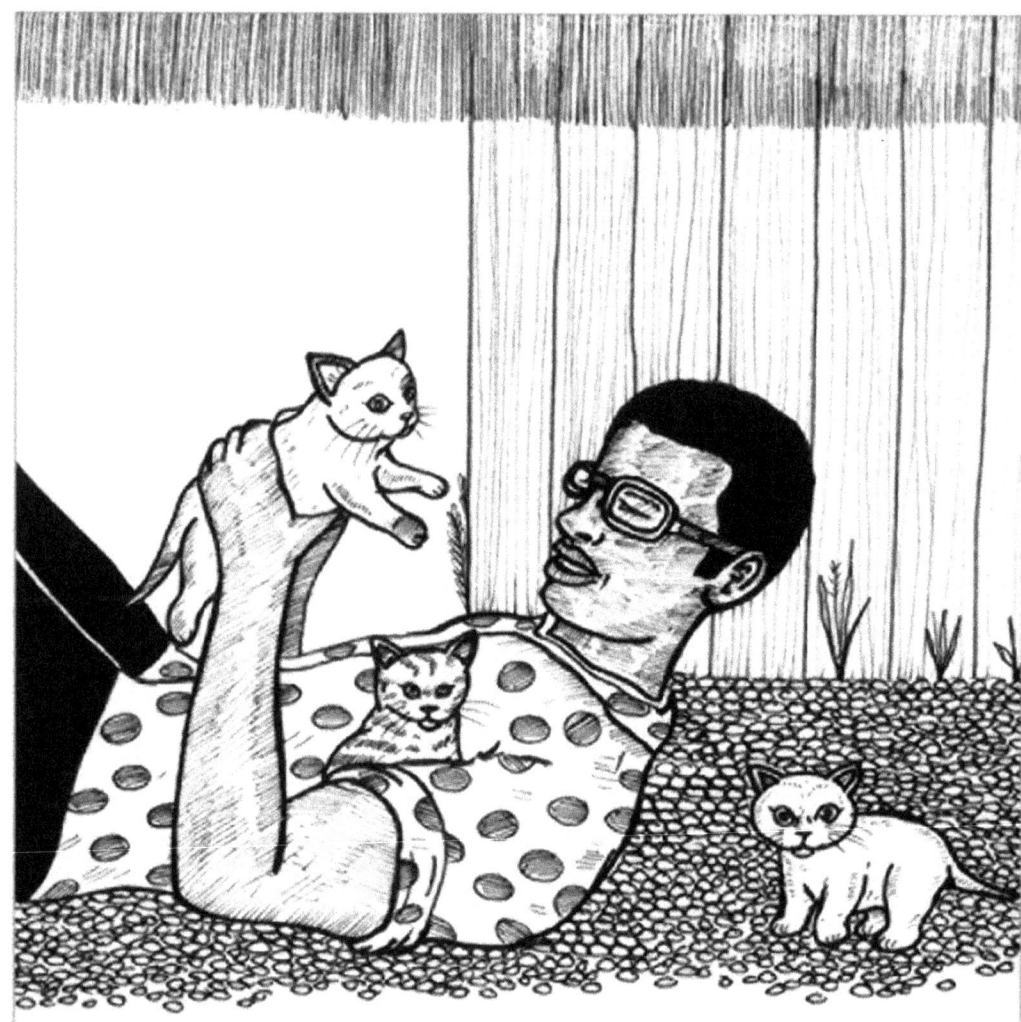

The resident who did not wish to be named said in a statement that they could not be certain that the man playing with the kittens in the yard did not also have a knife.

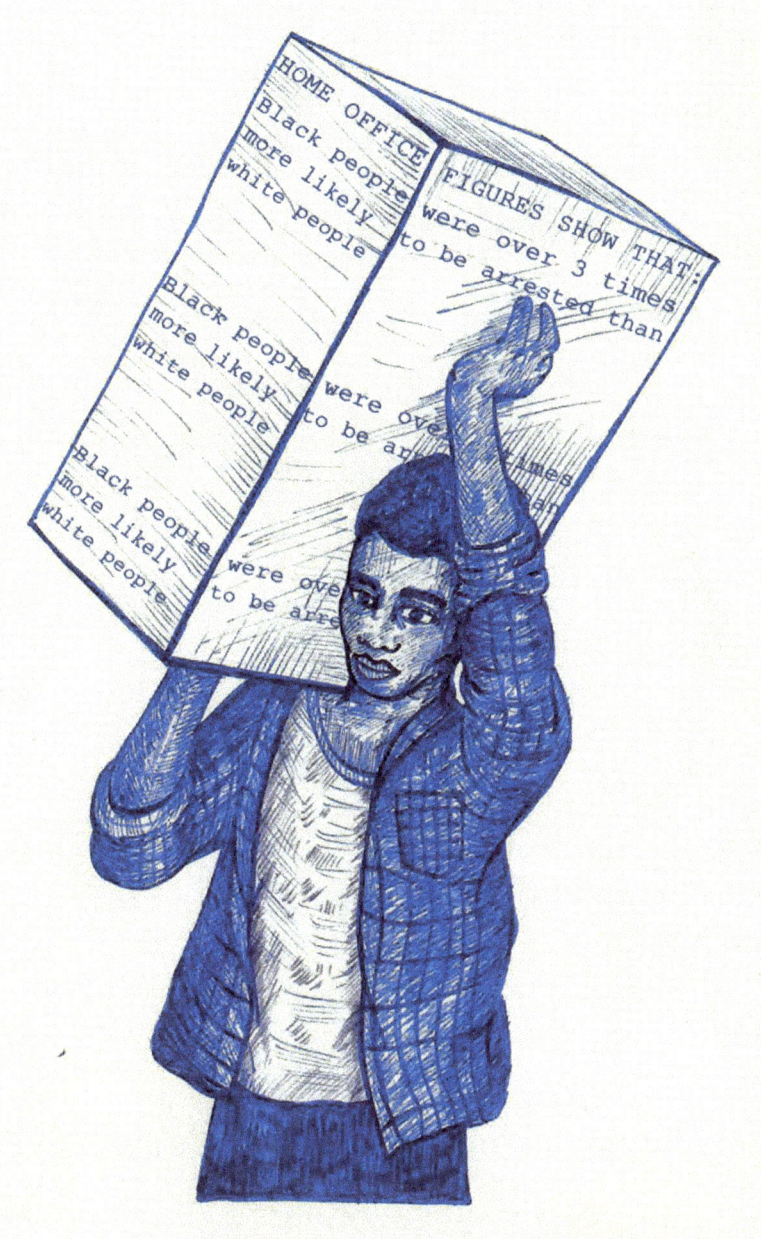

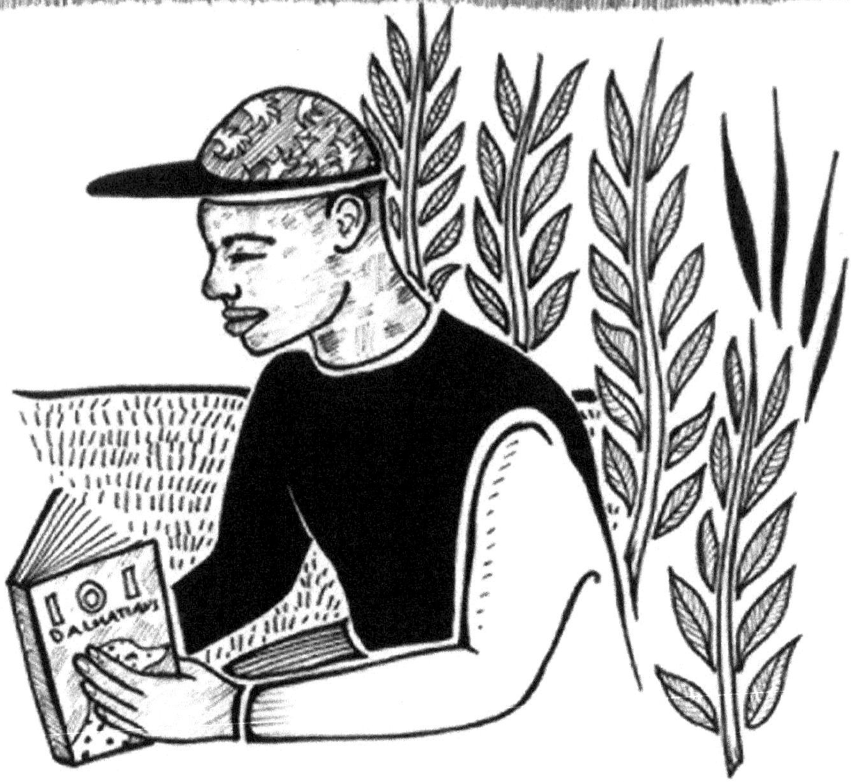

It was reported last night that an unaccompanied young man was spotted in a local public garden reading the book 101 dalmatians. The man described as of African Caribbean appearance first raised suspicion as he did not appear to be in possession of a dalmatian.

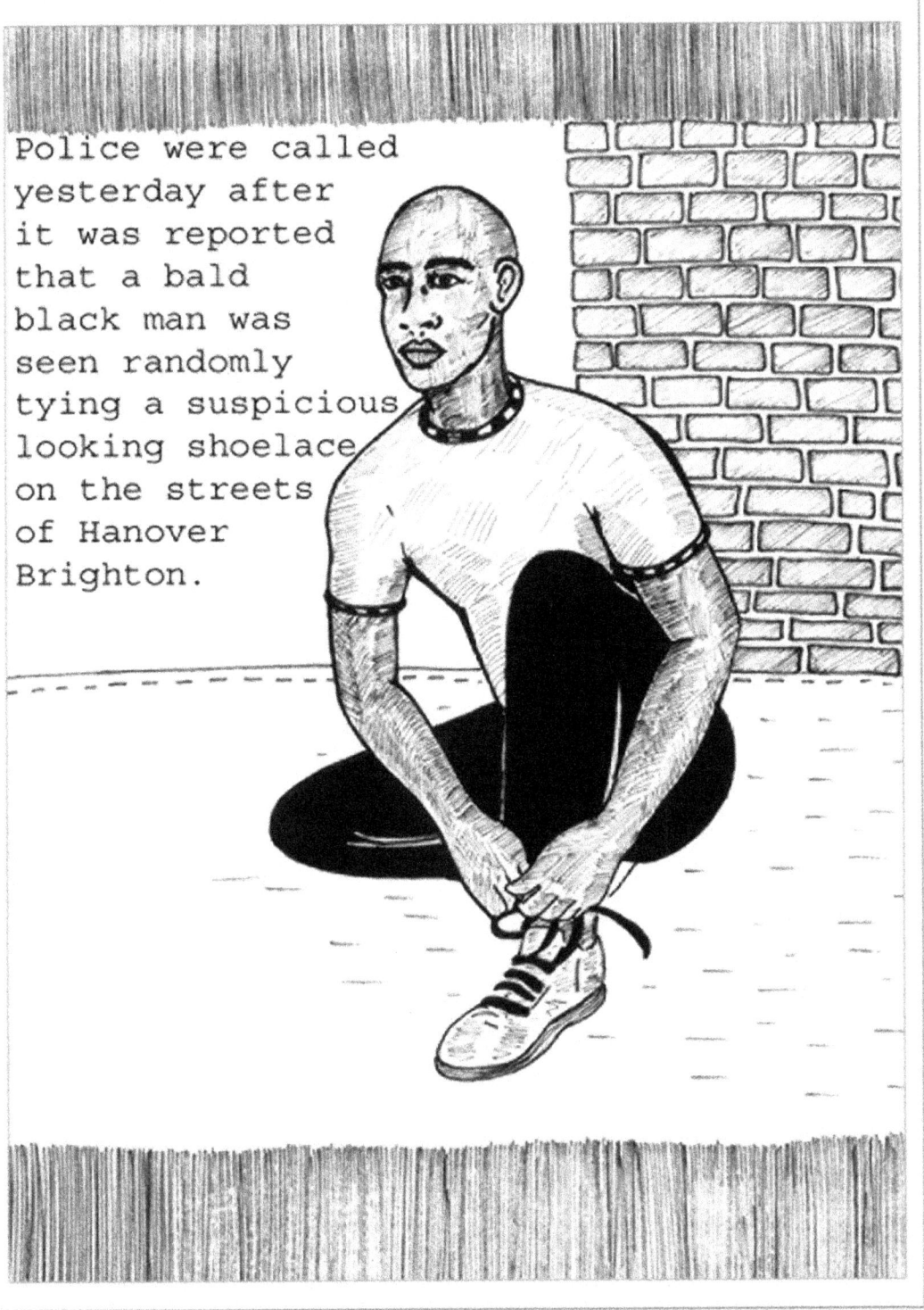

Police were called yesterday after it was reported that a bald black man was seen randomly tying a suspicious looking shoelace on the streets of Hanover Brighton.

The forest ended. Glad I was
To feel the light, and hear the hum
Of bees, and smell the drying grass
And the sweet mint, because I had come
To an end of forest, and because
Here was both road and inn, the sum
Of what's not forest. But 'twas here
They asked me if I did not pass
Yesterday this way? "Not you? Queer."
"Who then? and slept here?" I felt fear.

I learnt his road and, ere they were
Sure I was I, left the dark wood
Behind, kestrel and woodpecker,
The inn in the sun, the happy mood
When first I tasted sunlight there.
I travelled fast, in hopes I should
Outrun that other. What to do
When caught, I planned not. I pursued
To prove the likeness, and, if true,
To watch until myself I knew.

I tried the inns that evening
Of a long gabled high-street grey,
Of courts and outskirts, travelling
An eager but a weary way,
In vain. He was not there. Nothing
Told me that ever till that day
Had one like me entered those doors,
Save once. That time I dared: "You may
Recall"—but never-foamless shores
Make better friends than those dull boors.

Many and many a day like this
Aimed at the unseen moving goal

And nothing found but remedies
For all desire. These made not whole;
They sowed a new desire, to kiss
Desire's self beyond control,
Desire of desire. And yet
Life stayed on within my soul.
One night in sheltering from the wet
I quite forgot I could forget.

A customer, then the landlady
Stared at me. With a kind of smile
They hesitated awkwardly:
Their silence gave me time for guile.
Had anyone called there like me,
I asked. It was quite plain the wile
Succeeded. For they poured out all.
And that was naught. Less than a mile
Beyond the inn, I could recall
He was like me in general.

He had pleased them, but I less.
I was more eager than before
To find him out and to confess,
To bore him and to let him bore.
I could not wait: children might guess
I had a purpose, something more
That made an answer indiscreet.
One girl's caution made me sore,
Too indignant even to greet
That other had we chanced to meet.

I sought then in solitude.
The wind had fallen with the night; as still
The roads lay as the ploughland rude,
Dark and naked, on the hill.

BY: EDWARD THOMAS

Had there been ever any feud
'Twixt earth and sky, a mighty will
Closed it: the crocketed dark trees,
A dark house, dark impossible
Cloud-towers, one star, one lamp, one peace
Held on an everlasting lease:
And all was earth's, or all was sky's;
No difference endured between
The two. A dog barked on a hidden rise;
A marshbird whistled high unseen;
The latest waking blackbird's cries
Perished upon the silence keen.
The last light filled a narrow firth
Among the clouds. I stood serene,
And with a solemn quiet mirth,
An old inhabitant of earth.

Once the name I gave to hours
Like this was melancholy, when
It was not happiness and powers
Coming like exiles home again,
And weaknesses quitting their bowers,
Smiled and enjoyed, far off from men,
Moments of everlastingness.
And fortunate my search was then
While what I sought, nevertheless,
That I was seeking, I did not guess.
That time was brief: once more at inn
And upon road I sought my man
Till once amid a tap-room's din
Loudly he asked for me, began
To speak, as if it had been a sin,
Of how I thought and dreamed and ran
After him thus, day after day:
He lived as one under a ban
For this: what had I got to say?

I said nothing, I slipped away.

And now I dare not follow after
Too close. I try to keep in sight,
Dreading his frown and worse his laughter.
I steal out of the wood to light;
I see the swift shoot from the rafter
By the inn door: ere I alight
I wait and hear the starlings wheeze
And nibble like ducks: I wait his flight.
He goes: I follow: no release
Until he ceases. Then I also shall cease.

Source: Last Poems (1918)[1]

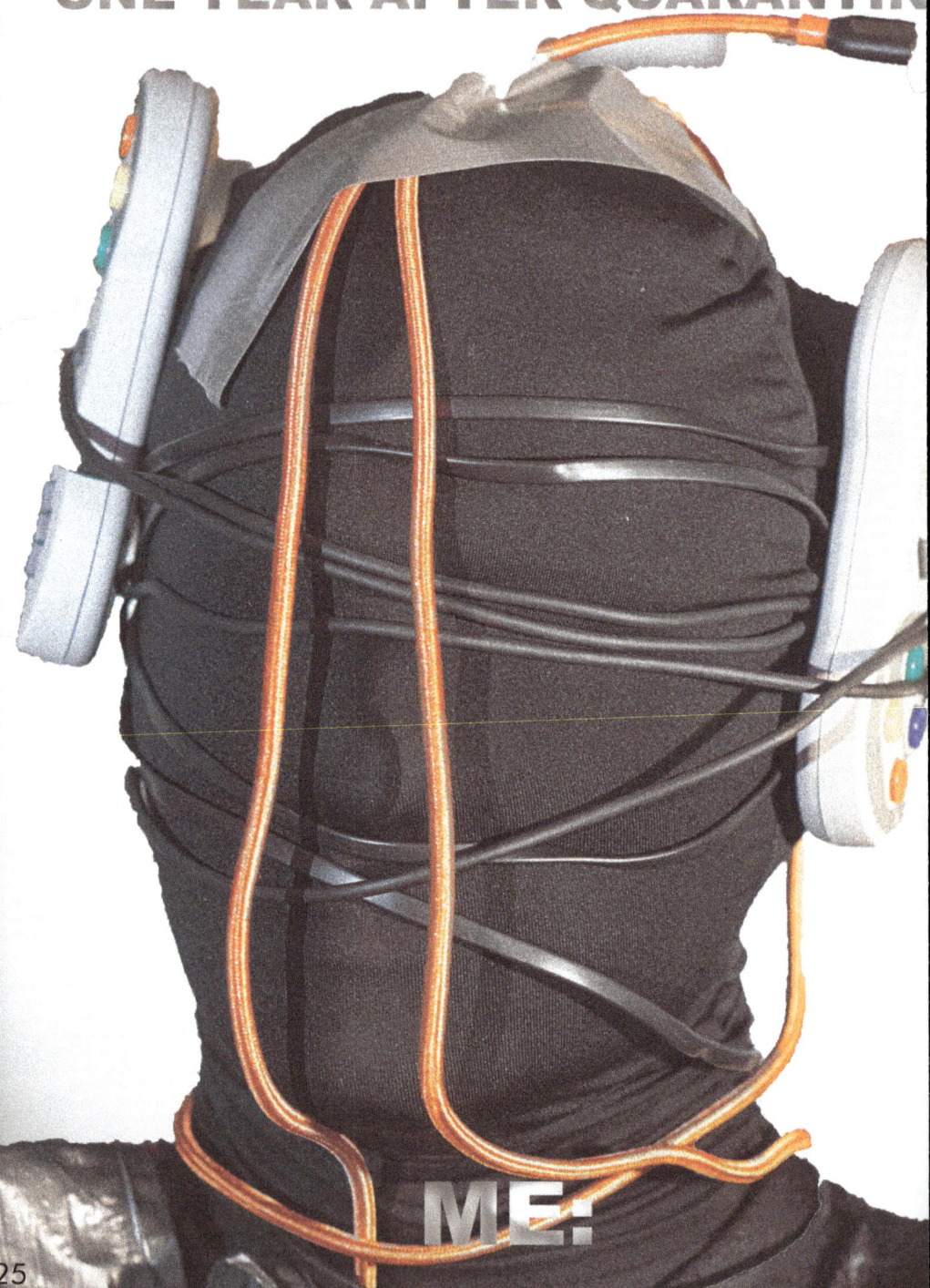

ME:

L'ENFANT
L'ENFANT
L'ENFANT
L'ENFANT
L'ENFANT
L'ENFANT

My name is l'enfant I'm a contemporary Artist living in Berlin. I started my career 5 years ago in London. I decided to start my utopia in the UK since I was given the opportunity to move there. I've taken this opportunity and started this project l'enfant. In the beginning I didn't really know where to start or how to start. I started with graffiti and physical installations I glued on the walls of London. Later I included photography and then the styling came naturally. I'm currently working in 8 different mediums. I don't want to limit myself with l'enfant and decided not to put myself in a box and represent as an artist all fields im working on. Paintings, styling photography, installations, music , video. After exploring my art style and evolving my utopia I decided to move to Berlin. Brexit and the pandemic forced me to change my life again.

@lenfant_

I created everything out of spontaneous nature. All my work is done with an intuitive
naive approach. I never work with concepts.

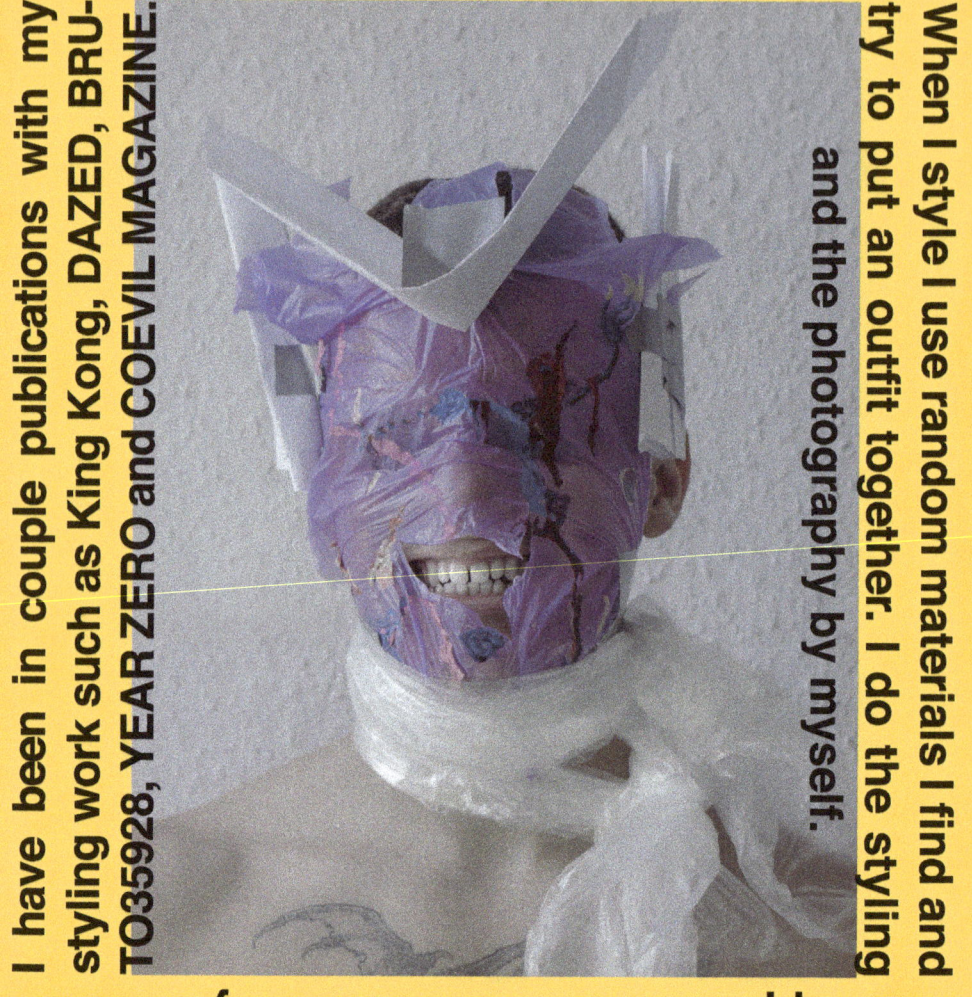

I have been in couple publications with my
styling work such as King Kong, DAZED, BRU-
TO35928, YEAR ZERO and COEVIL MAGAZINE.

When I style I use random materials I find and
try to put an outfit together. I do the styling
and the photography by myself.

I use my friends as models and I
approach an anti fashion style.

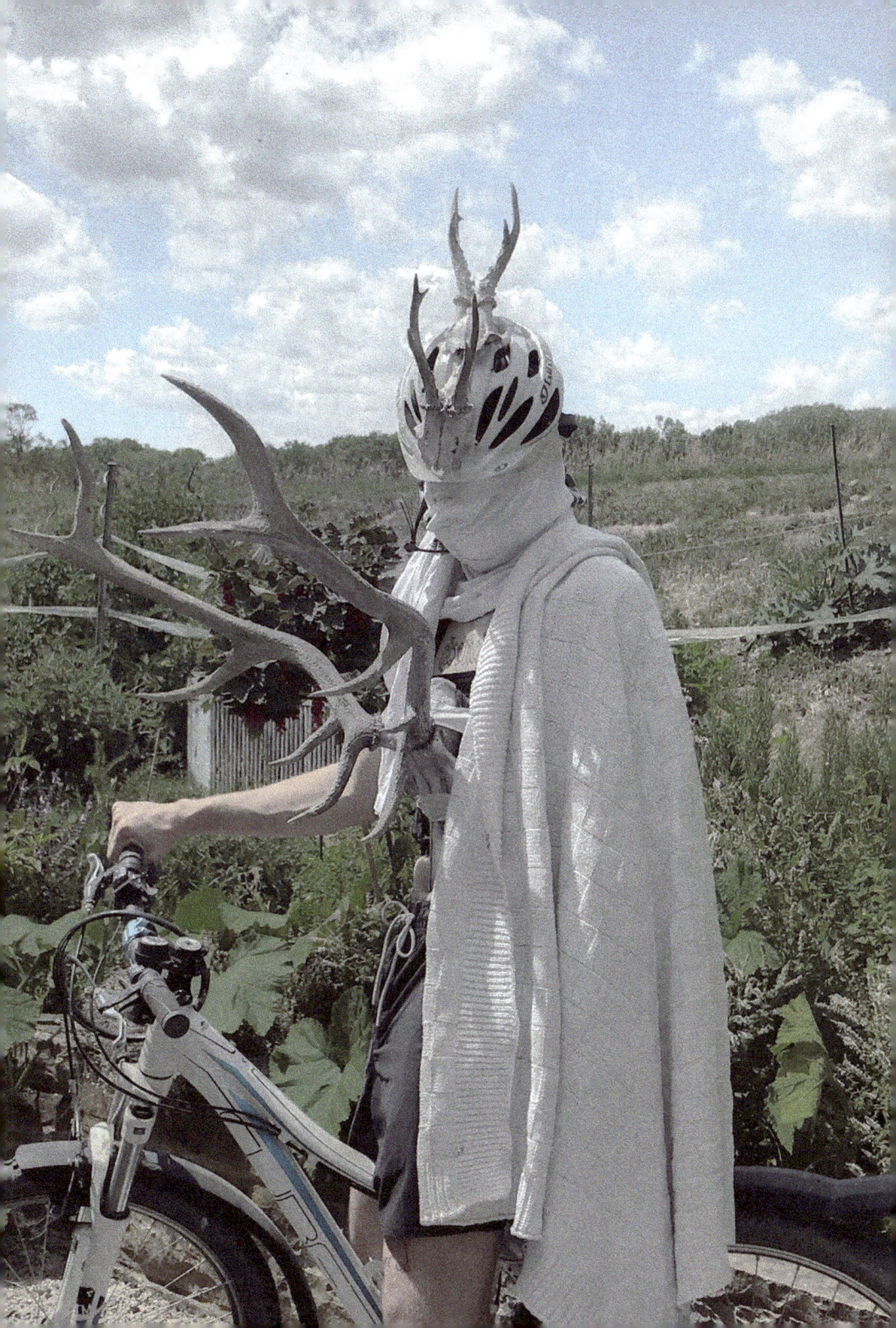

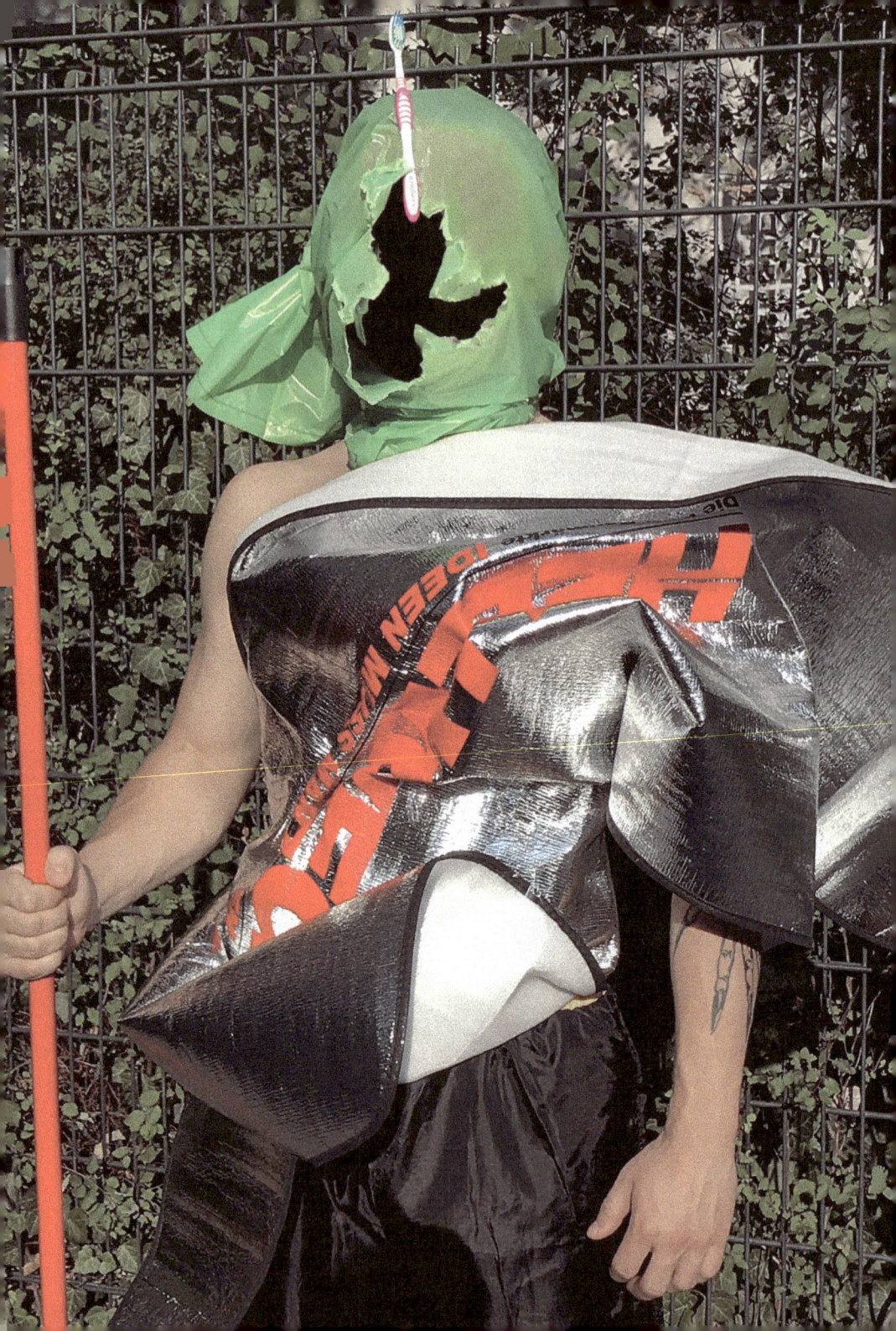

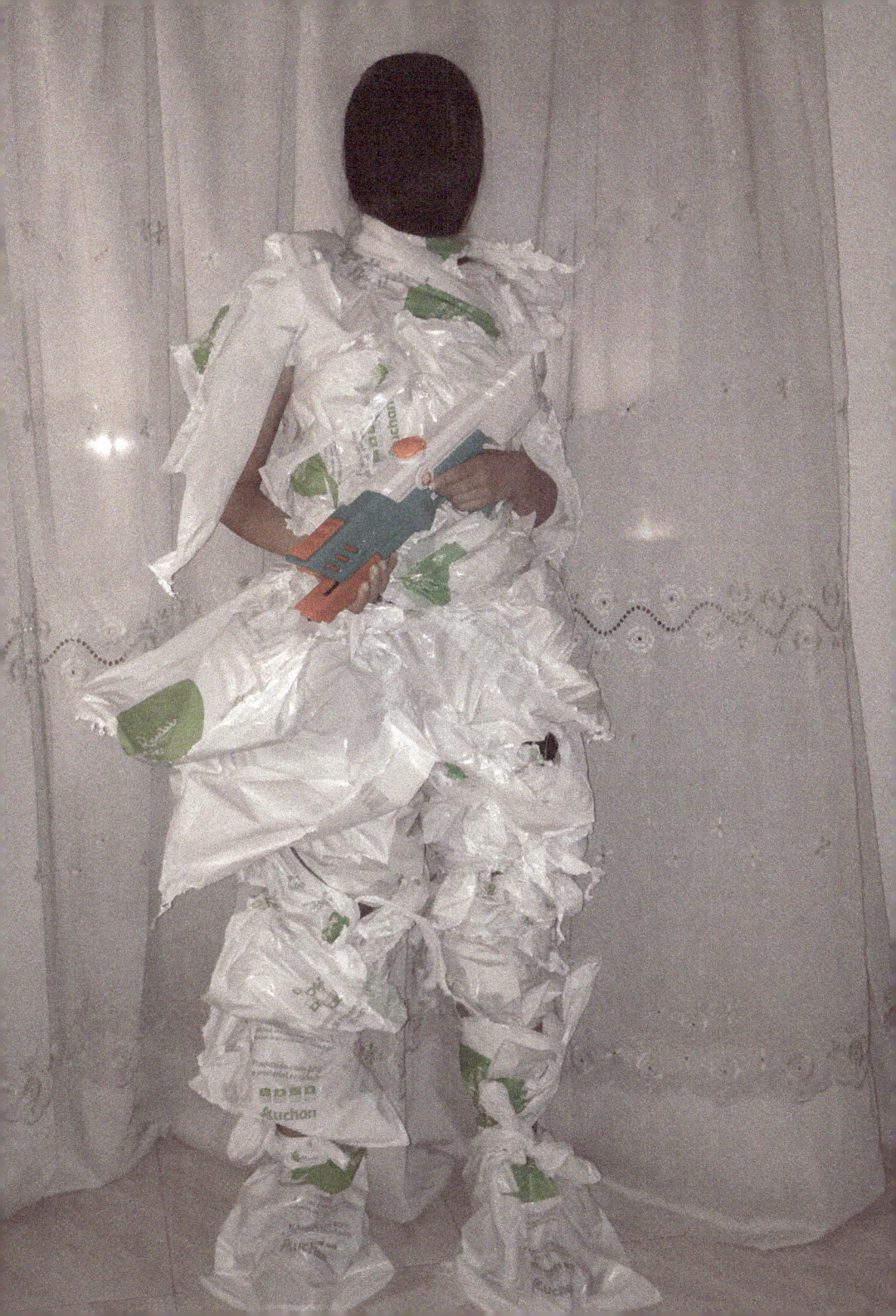

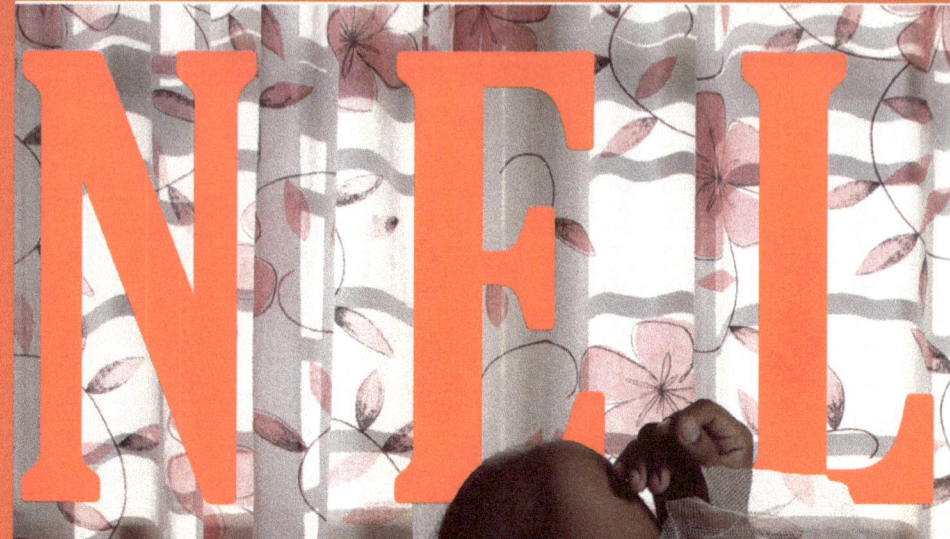

NEL

Since 2008 Nelson Morales has dedicated himself completely to photography independently and has studied various educational programs of contemporary photography in Mexico. His work focuses mainly on issues of gender, body, identity and
sexual diversity.

He has made various collectives in 20 countries and he has obtained different mentions and recognitions around the world. His work has been published in Aperture, New York times, Vogue Italia, Vogue México, Vice, TETU, Loeil de la photograpie, The British Journal of photography and others. In 2018 he published his first Photobook, "Musas Muxe" and in 2019 he published his second Photobook "Fantastic Woman".

MOR

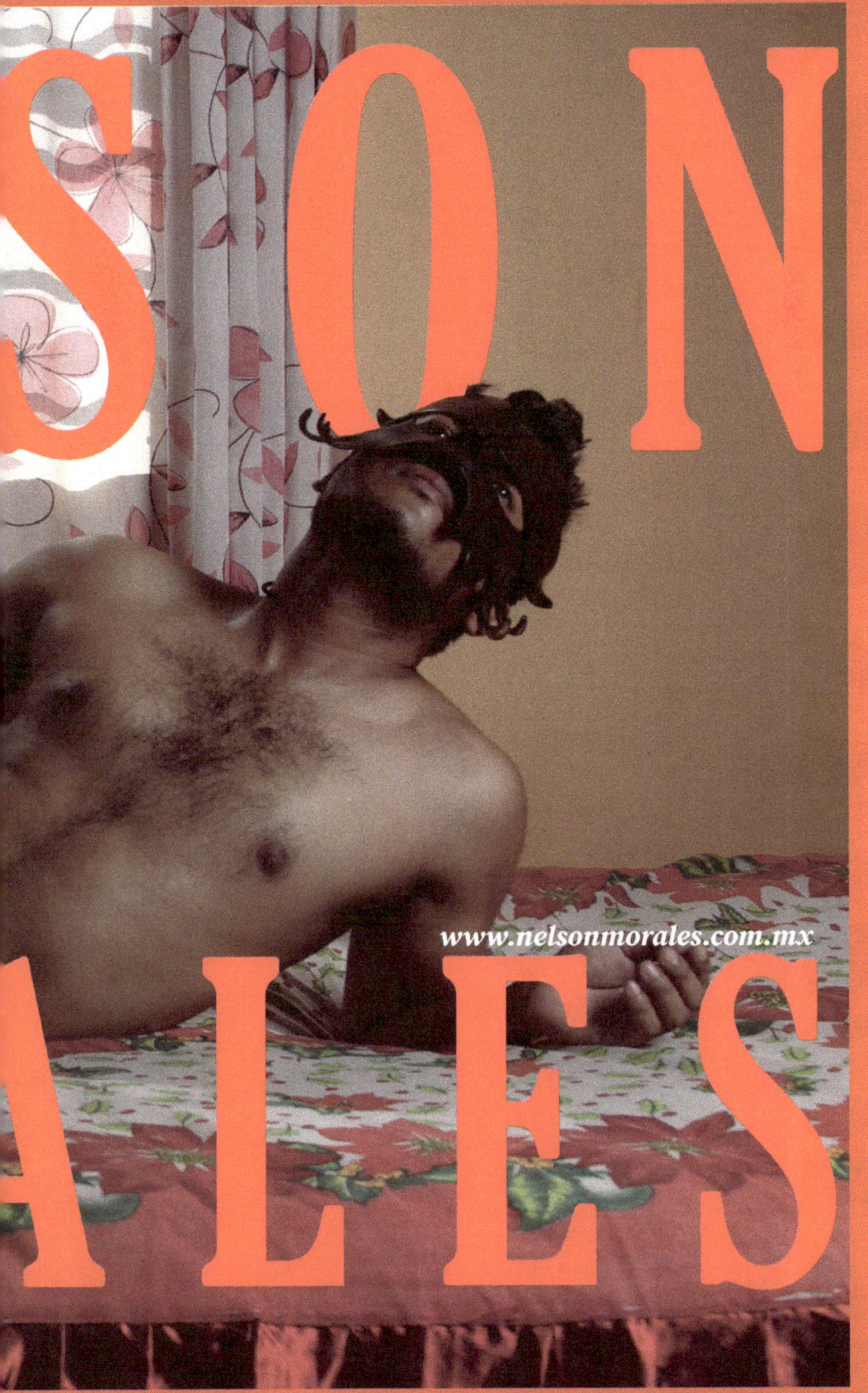

www.nelsonmorales.com.mx

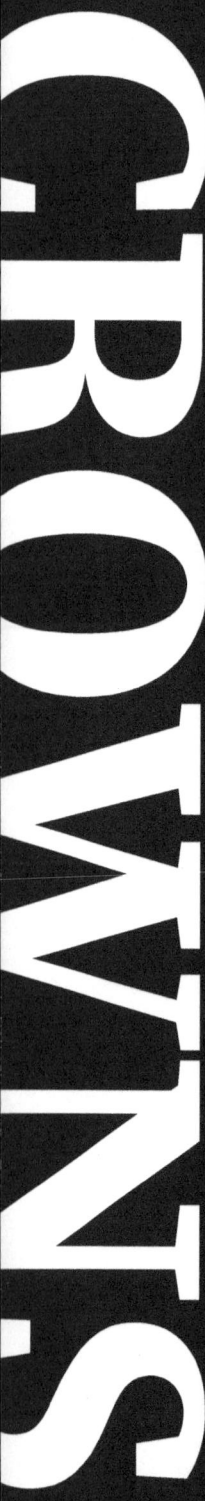

Since I was a child, I had this fascination for beauty pageants, especially pageant crowns, their symbols and meanings, their beauty, and the variety of them in different cultures. I have previously been portraying transvestite and transgender beauty queens in **Muxe** culture and was struck by their obsession with becoming a beauty queen. This series is a sequel of **I WANT TO BE A QUEEN**, however they are more introspective and conceptual images where the play of colors, fabrics, shapes, imagination and mystery seduces us.

Behind the fabrics and shapes are hidden stories of life, longing, and fantasies in which all of us at some point in our lives have dreamed of.

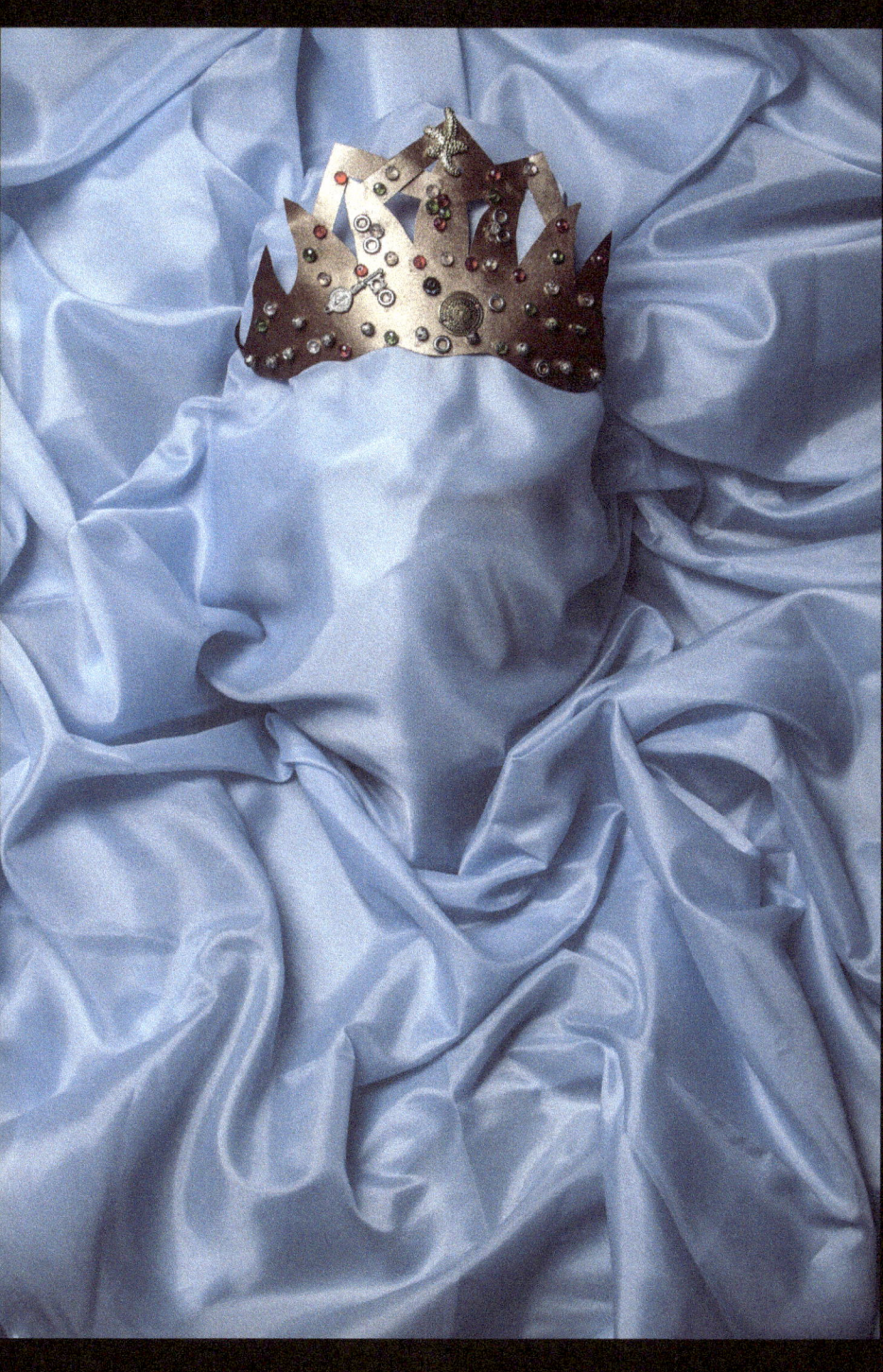

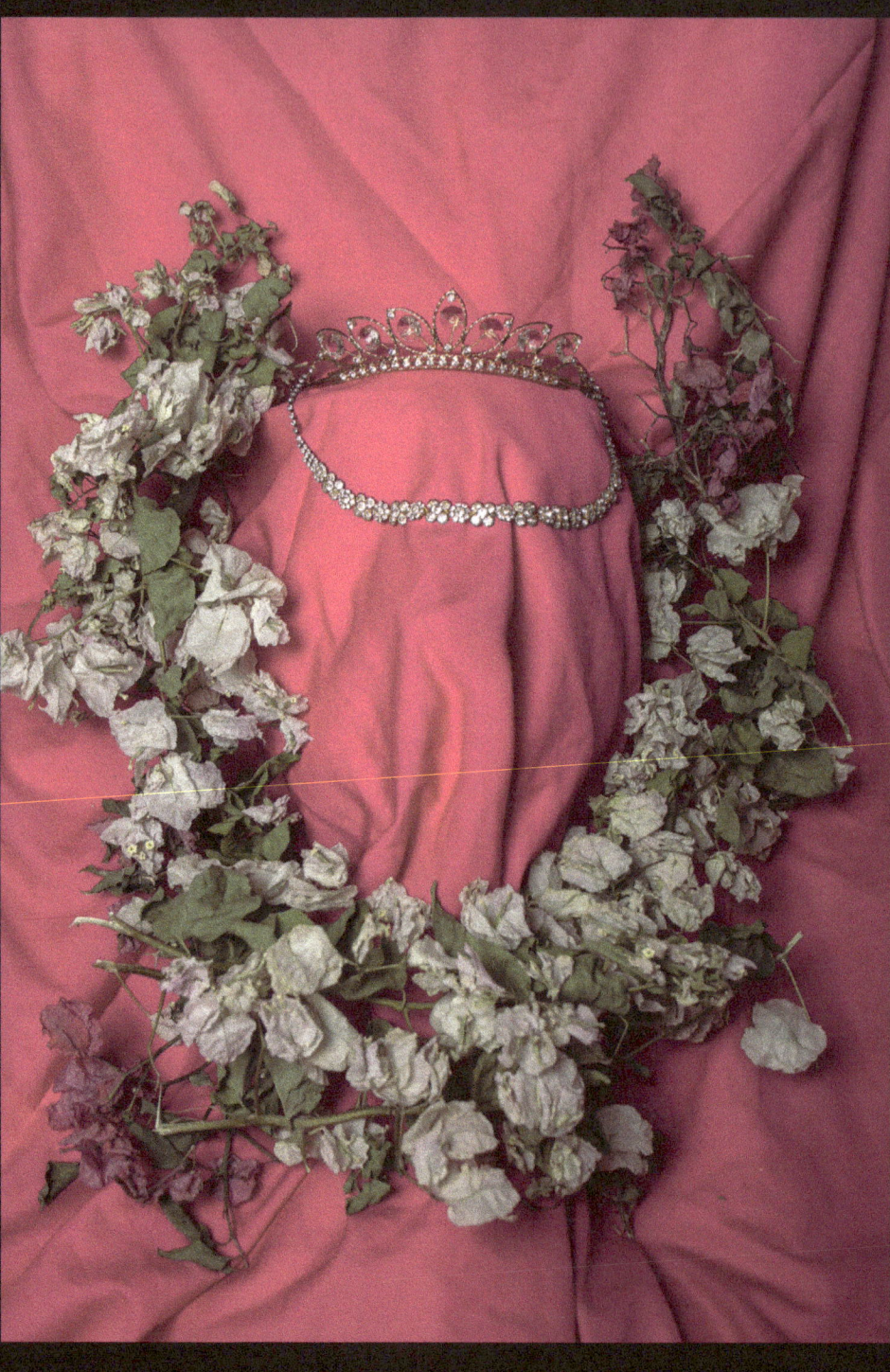

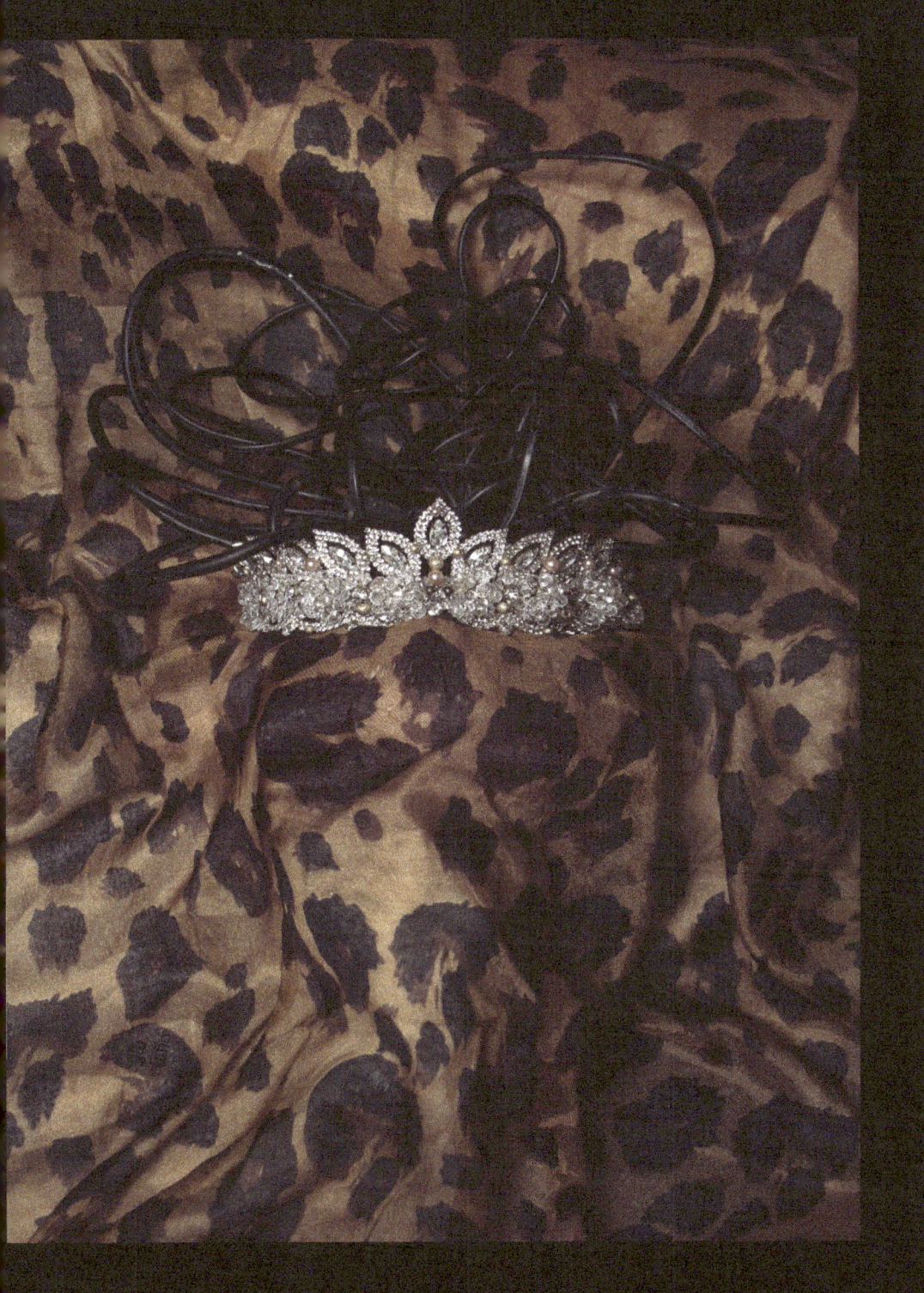

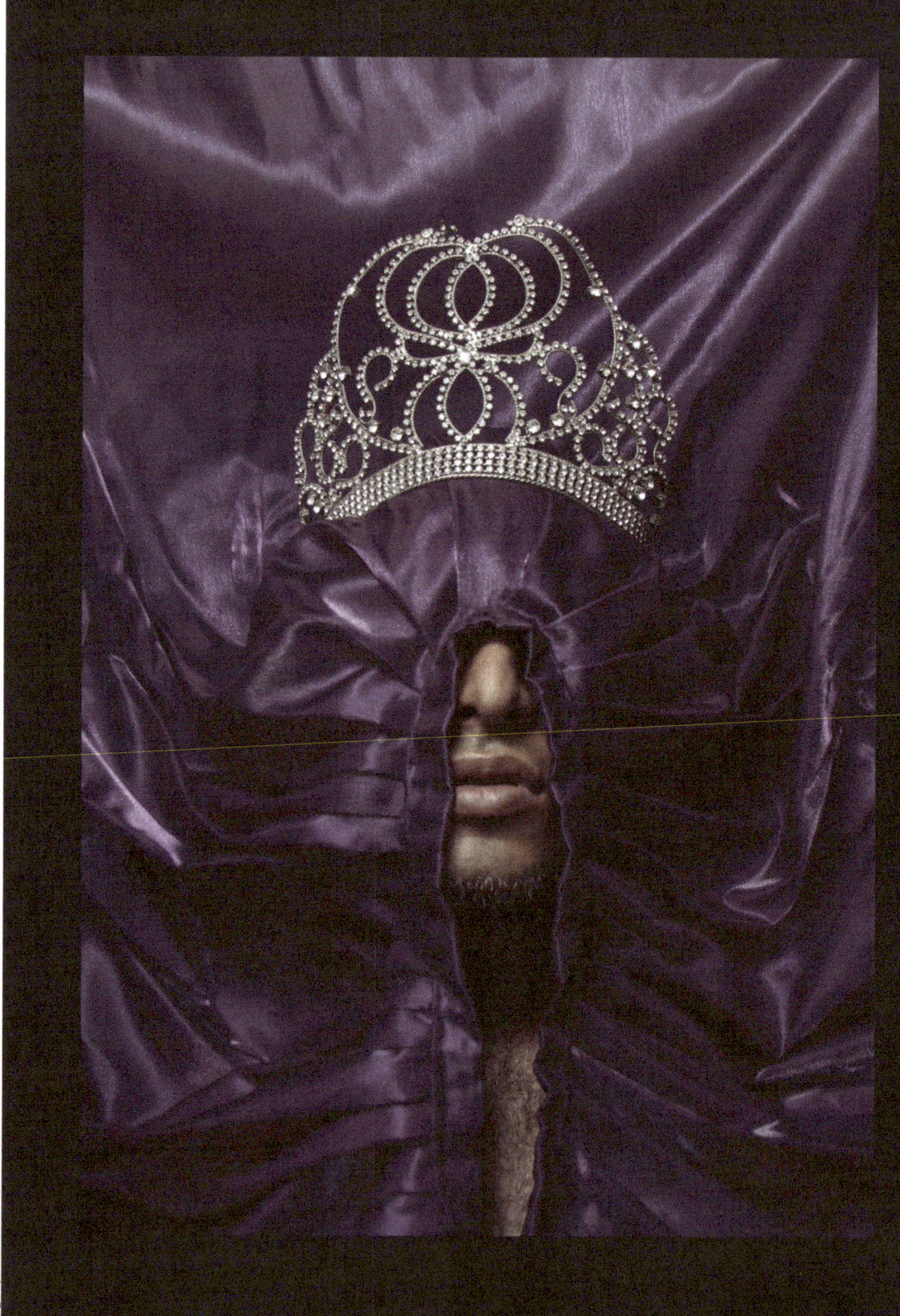

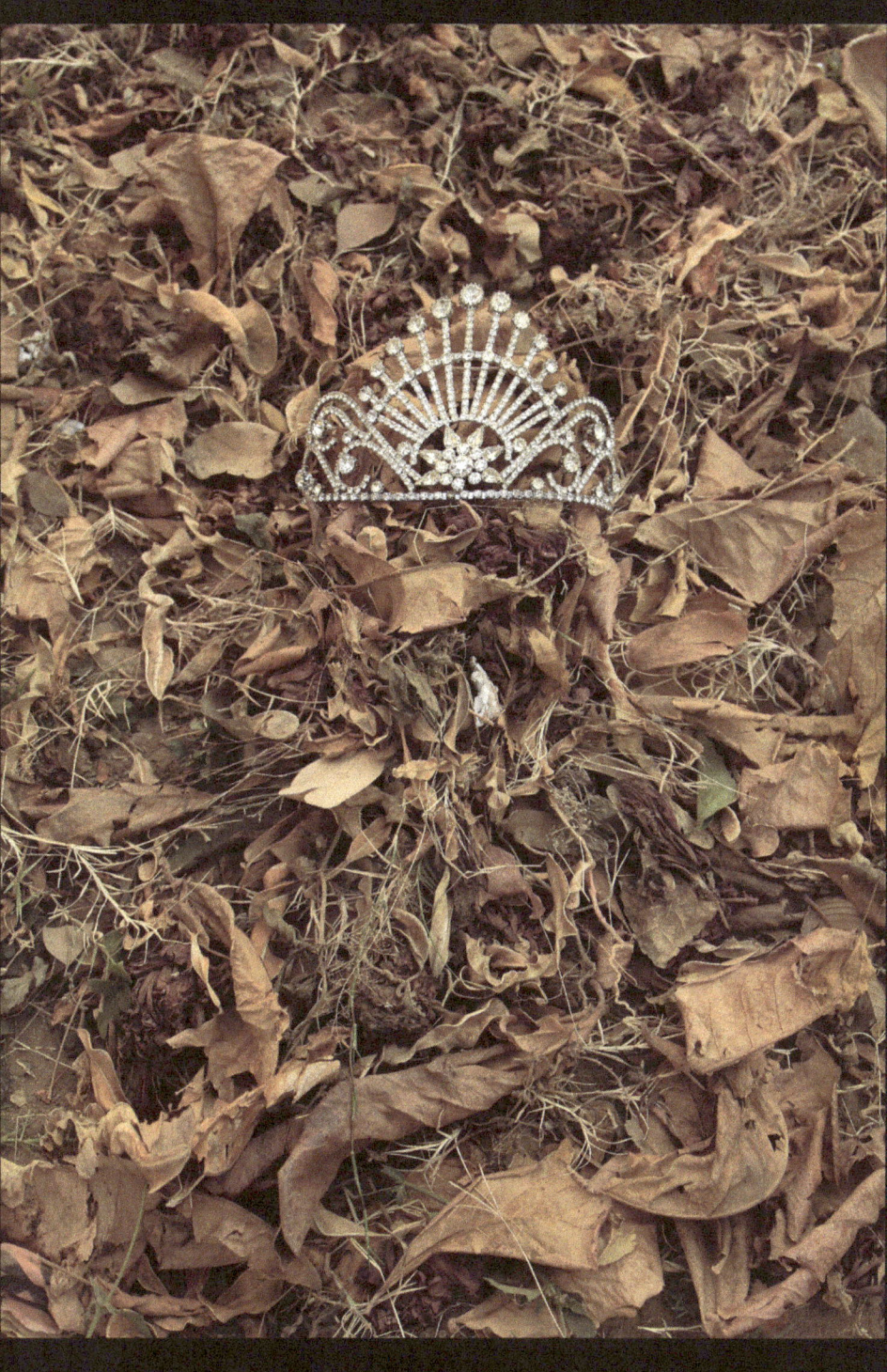

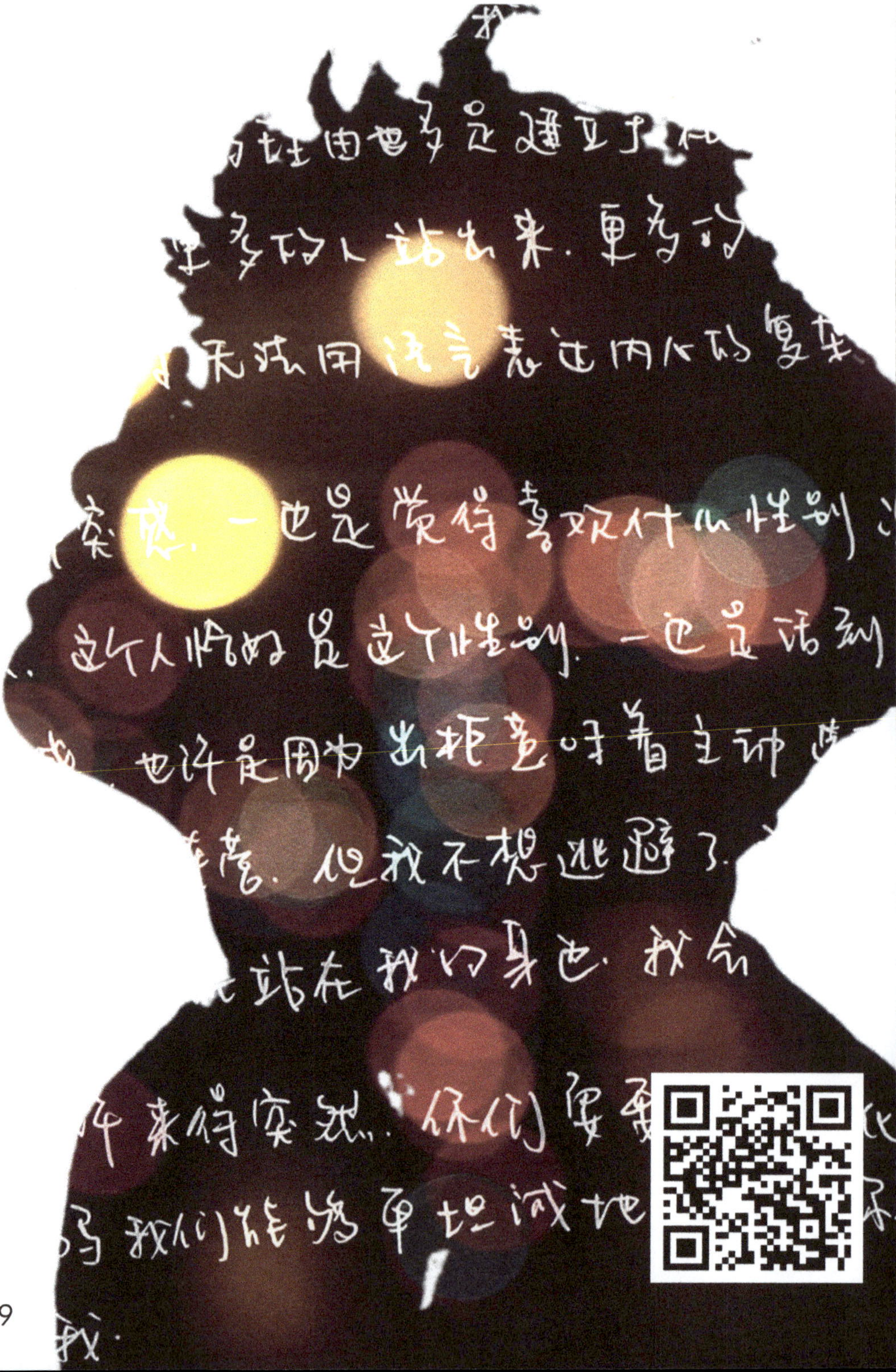

男性由...是通过了...

生多的人站出来. 更多的

...天试用语言表达内心的复杂

...然. 一也是觉得喜欢什么性别...

...这个人怀疑是这个性别. 一也是活到...

...也许是用...出柜...着主动...

...意. 但我不想逃避了.

...站在我的身边. 我会

...来得突然. 你们要...

...我们能够...减地...

我.

Mengwen Cao is a photographer, multimedia artist, and cultural organizer. Born and raised in China, they are based in New York. As a queer immigrant, they use care and tenderness to explore spaces between race, gender, and cultural identity. As a board member of Authority Collective and a founding member of Chinese Storytellers, they are championing diverse narratives and perspectives in the media industry.

Their projects have been featured in publications like The New York Times, The New Yorker, NPR, Foreign Policy, The Guardian, Sina, Tencent. They have participated in international exhibitions like Photoville, Jimei Arles, Lianzhou Foto Festival.

Mengwen graduated from the New Media Narratives and Documentary Practice program at the International Center of Photography. They received NLGJA's Excellence in Photojournalism Award in 2019. They were recognized by The Lit List in 2018 and PDN 30 New and Emerging Photographers to Watch in 2019.

MENGWEN CAO

@mengwencao
www.mengwencao.com/hereweare

HERE WE ARE

My parents thought I had never been in love. We didn't talk about relationships because I had a secret: I like girls.

I created a video letter coming out to them and shared it with them as we talked on Facetime.

Only around 5 percent of LGBTQ people in China are completely open about their identity due to huge family and societal pressure.

This project aims to share raw and intimate moments and adding to nuanced stories about Chinese queer community.

Here we are in spite of everything.

I HAVE A SECRET

My name is Meng.

I'm a 25-year-old Chinese girl.
My parents think I have never fallen in love.
We don't talk about relationships, because I **have a secret:**
I like girls.

As much as I want my family to know me better, the fear stops me from revealing the truth.
I wrote a letter to my parents.

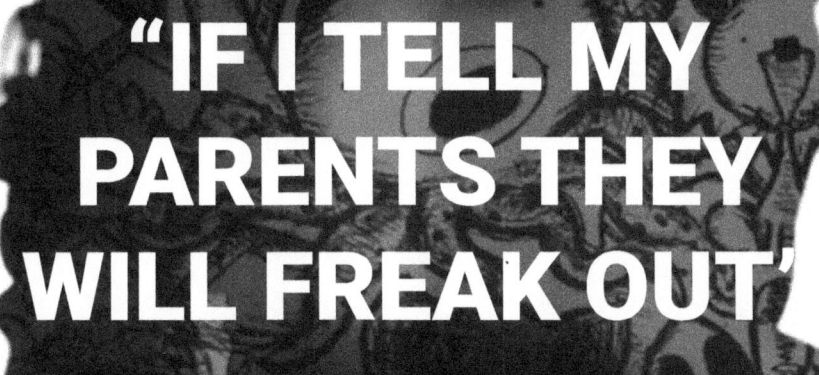

MY STORY IS NOT UNIQUE

Fully out   Partially Out   Not Out

Less than 5.5 percent of LGBTQ individuals in China choose to be fully open regarding their sexual orientation or gender identity

April 11, 2016

I CAN'T LIE ANYMORE

Four months after I wrote my coming out letter and made
that video, I decided to show it to my parents via Facetime

WHAT ABOUT KIDS?
DO YOU HAVE ANYONE YOU LIKE NOW?
ARE YOU JUST CURIOUS?
DO YOU THINK IT IS BECAUSE YOU ARE IN THE ART CIRCLE?
ARE YOU REALLY SURE?
ARE YOU THE MAN OR THE WOMAN IN A RELATIONSHIP?
HAVE YOU EVER LIKED A BOY?
WHO WILL TAKE CARE OF YOU WHEN YOU ARE OLDER?
WHAT'S YOUR PLAN IF YOU COME BACK TO CHINA?
DO YOU THINK YOU ARE JUST INFLUENCES BY WESTERN CULTURE?

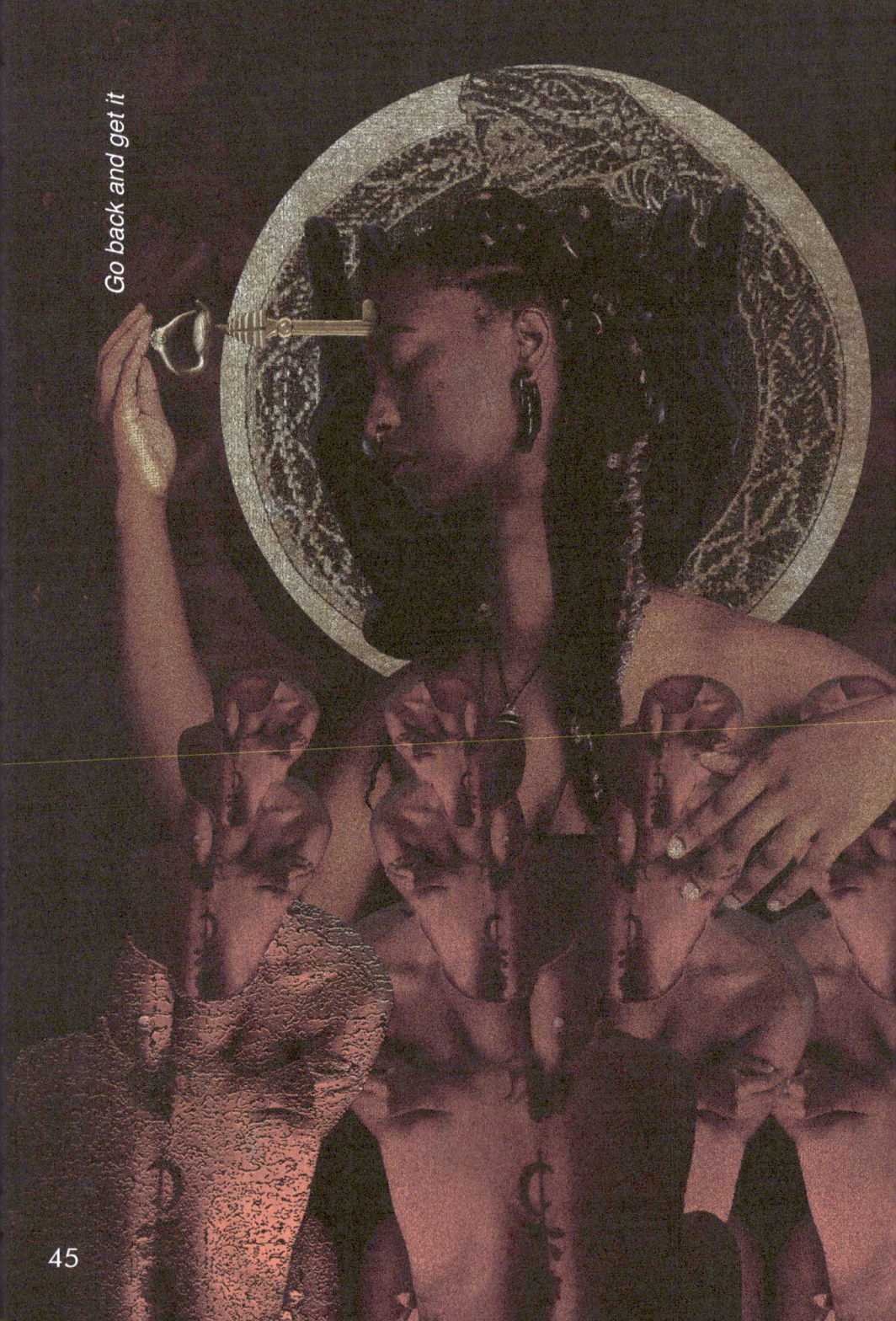

Go back and get it

ARIT
ETUKUDO

Arit Emmanuela Etukudo is a Nigerian-American self-portrait whose practice focuses on the simultaneous invisibility and hypervisibility of the self, body and existence. She earned her BA in Cinematic Arts and minor in Creative Writing from University of Maryland Baltimore County in 2016.

She then earned her MFA in Fine Art from Nottingham Trent University in 2019. During her MFA study she took an Erasmus at École Supérieure des Beaux-arts to expand her research. Her work has earned her achievements such as the 2019 NAE Future Exhibition Prize, the 2017 Indie Capitol Award for Best Experimental / Animated film, and the 2016 UMBC Senior Exhibition prize for Outstanding Work in Cinematic Arts.

@arit_emmanuela

www.redbubble.com/people/AritEmmanuela

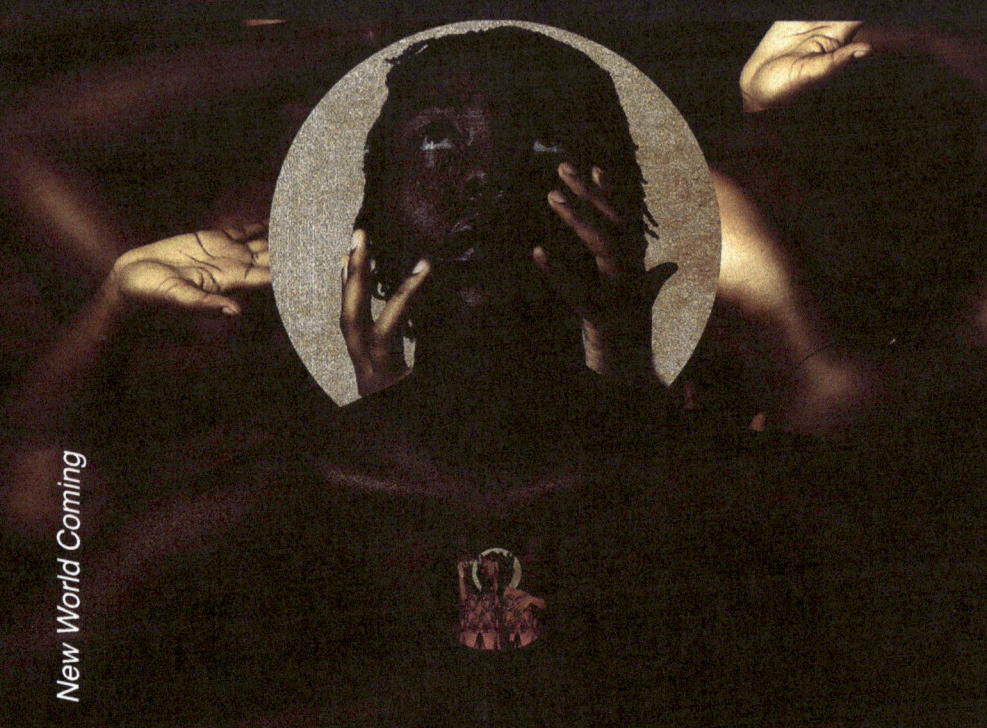

New World Coming

As an experimental storyteller, Arit Emmanuela Etukudo recreates the relationship between her body's physical movements in the world and its incorporeal movements as a result of that. In her work, her body is not limited by form, space or time; but instead manifests itself beyond what is immediately perceptible.

The deconstruction of the known world and the act of her identity being the holder of dimension challenges the modern constructs of how the black body is allowed to exist. This inserts the narrative of Afrofuturism, as a source of black radical imagination and Afrofrequency, the root of the black magical experience. Her work acts as a source of emancipation from systems that attempt to limit her existence. Inspired by creators like Zanele Muholi, Frida Kahlo, Bill Viola and Athi-Patra Ruga; Etukudo creates work that uses the body as language.

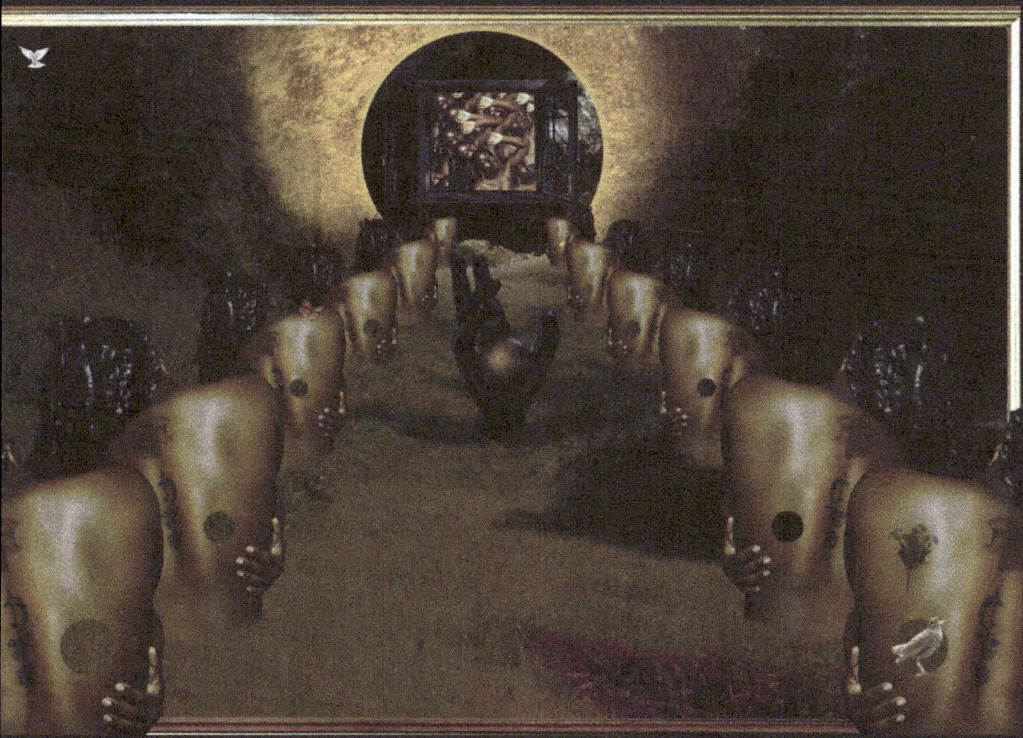

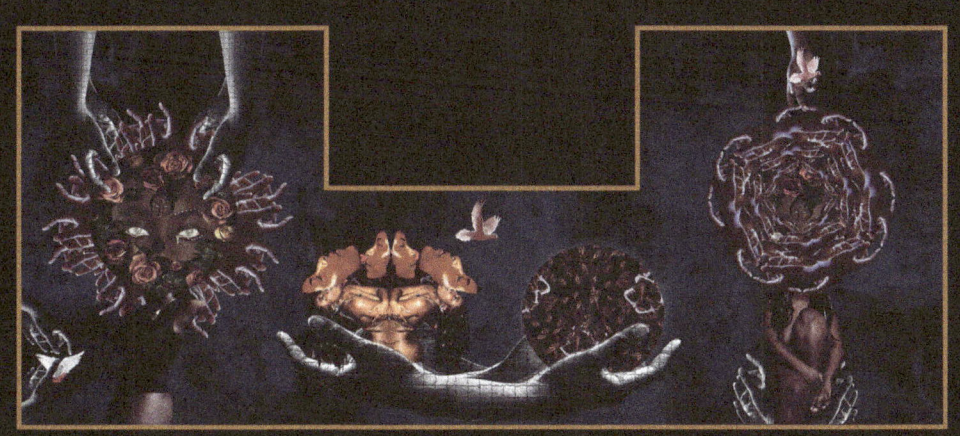

Self portrait thinking of all that has left me

I once was held for 1000 years.

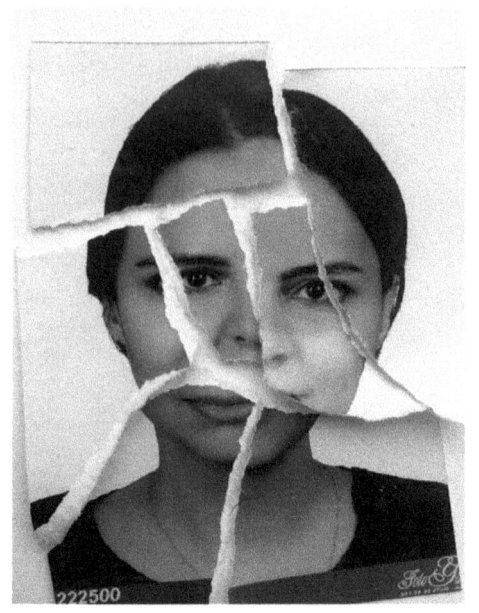

TUGBA TIRPAN

Tugba Tirpan is a Londan based artist-curator working across a range of artistic mediums including photography, video, performance and installation. Tugba's work often explores complex subject matters ranging from identity to mental health and their intersections with socio-political and economic system(s). She often employs conceptual ways of working to challenge and expose; power structures, hegemonic ideologies and binaries.

www.tugbatirpan.com

@tugba.tirpan

THE MOST FOREIGN LAND

'The Most Foreign Land, I' is a work in progress and it is the completed artwork. Consisting of three digital negative photographs, these chronological photos were taken as part of the creative process and were never meant to be exhibited. My personal migration history (and present) is tightly intertwined within these images. I eventually abandoned trying to compose the 'ideal' image envisaged in my mind. Instead, I embraced the process for what it is; imperfect but exuberant.

These images were taken on a makeshift backdrop, my bedsheets. They are out of focus, disproportionately framed and none are staged. The original print photographs were only a few among the many biometric photos I used for my multiple leave to remain permit renewals in the UK and my actors headshots I had taken during the same period.

'The Most Foreign Land, I' explores the multitude of identities, specifically the concept of a 'foreign identity' molded by the migration process. This piece entangles the creative process with the bureaucratic, revealing the emotional topography of an arcane experience along the way. Perhaps, it's a map of the ecologies of identity.

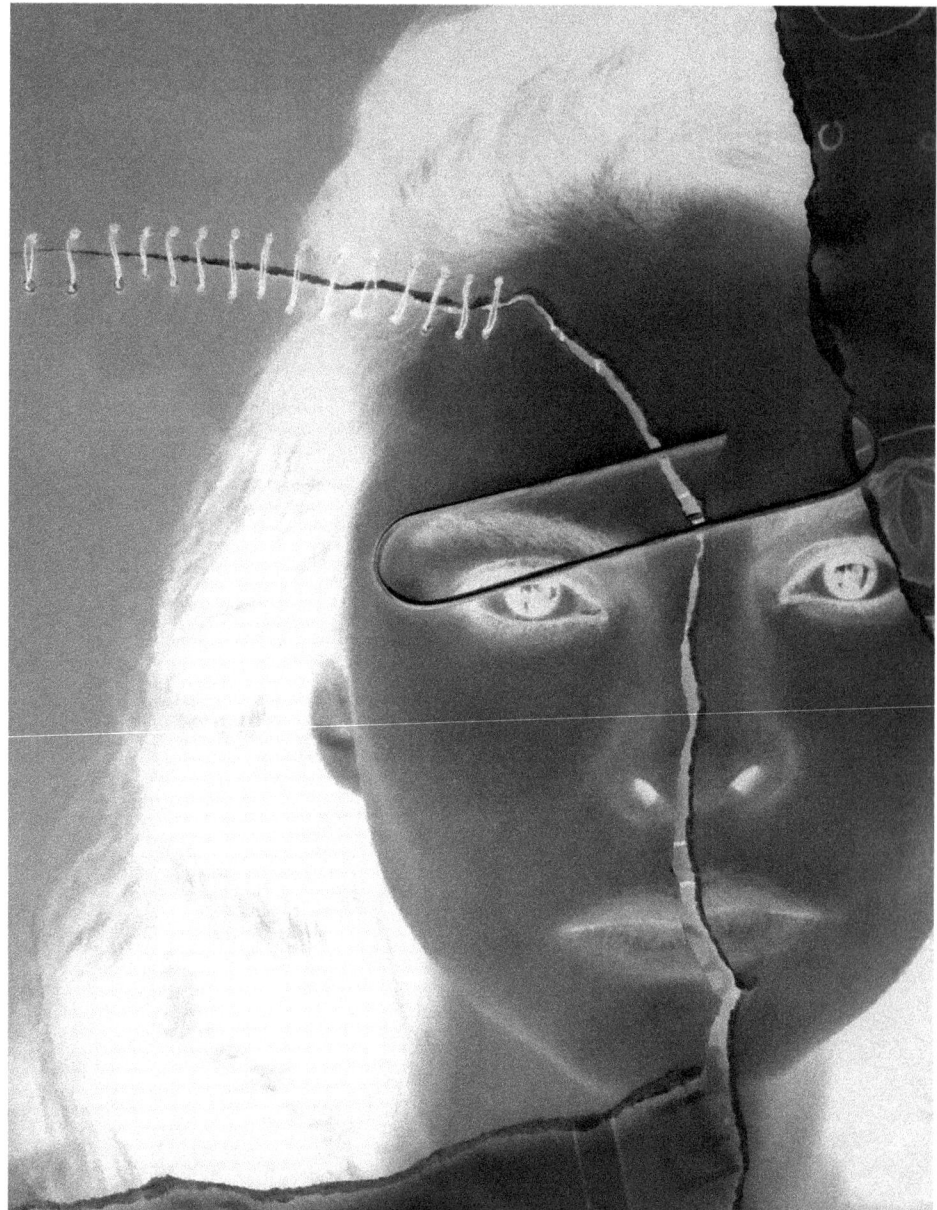

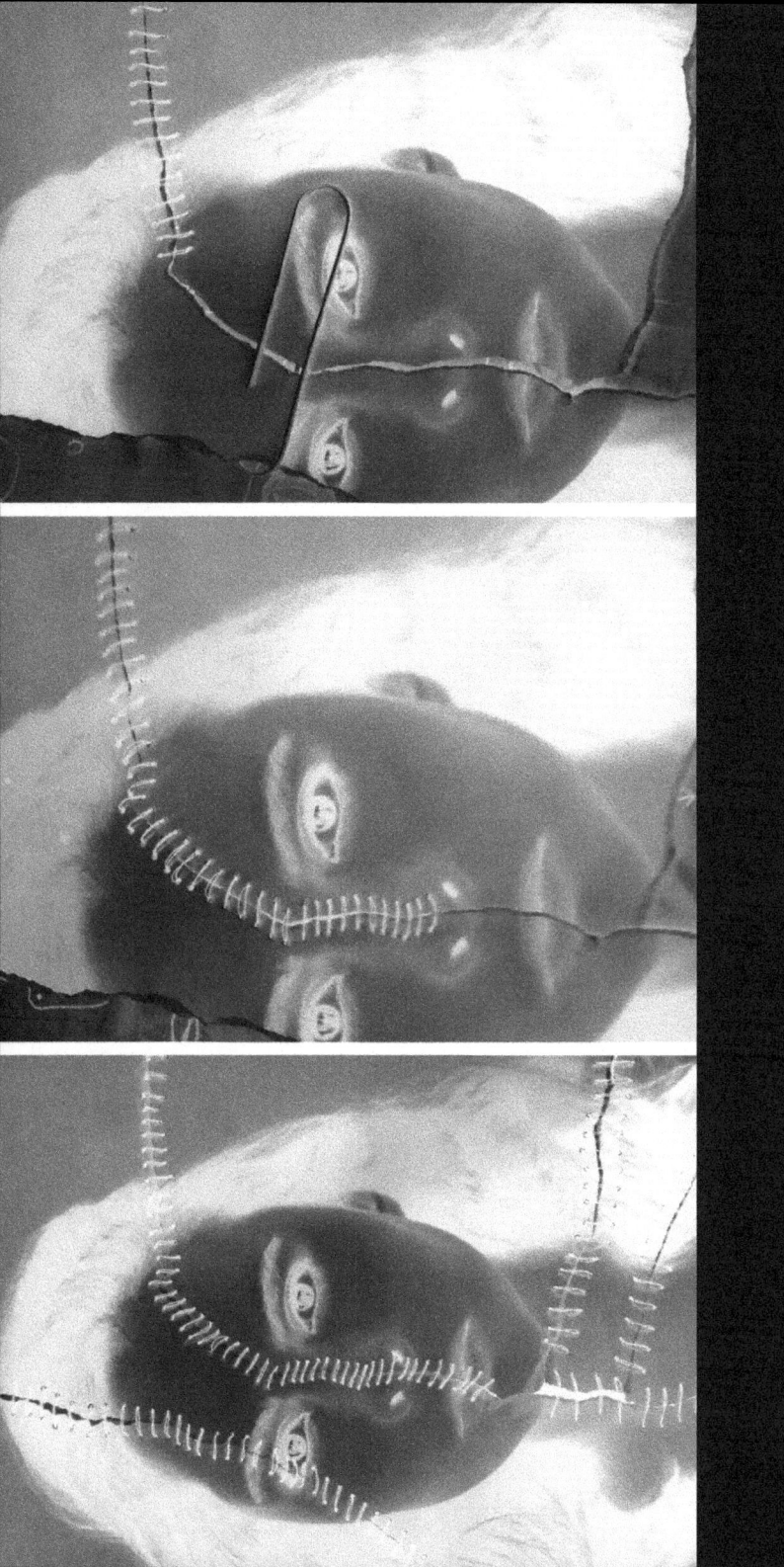

JENN NAS

Jenny Nash was born in Yorkshire in the North of England and grew up in the town of Garforth in Leeds. After their father's death when they were nine, Nash felt displaced, abandoned and isolated from other children. They sought the company of adults almost as if trying to find answers and comfort from the relentless bullying so often inflicted by other children and predominantly, perhaps more worryingly, high school teachers. Reflecting on their archive, it is clear to see that from a young age, their everyday documentary practice was how they process the external world and the images taken became an interface between that external world and their chaotic internal world. Nash began their relationship with a camera as a documentary photographer, using the lens as a tool to make sense of the place they were growing up (or trapped) in and to connect with others during their adolescent years. Consequently, their passion for documentary photography has taken them all over the UK. Nash does attempt to document specifically LGBTQ+ Pride and their work with Stand Up To Rac-

ism. This artist finds it a responsability to document the predominantly Bangladeshi Muslim community they now live in east London, portraying the people as the integrated, hard working members of the UK that they are. Nash sees this practice as using their privilege the best they can to amplify the voices of the BAME and LGBTQ+ community and break the media narrative that is driving their country to the political right in the wake of the Brexit travesty. Jenny Nash also uses the experiential nature of their photographic practice as an important component in their work. Nash merges her love for documentary with cathartic methods whilst documenting spaces of memory. They appropriate widely used therapeutic PTSD treatments such as returning to sites of past trauma accompanied by a psychotherapist. But this artist chooses to go alone, taking a camera instead. Alternatively, they confront past trauma in self portraiture sessions which enables them to access deep memories and converse with elements of their history thought to have been abandoned to the unconscious. This artists derived their own practice methodology of Solo-Phototherapy from the work

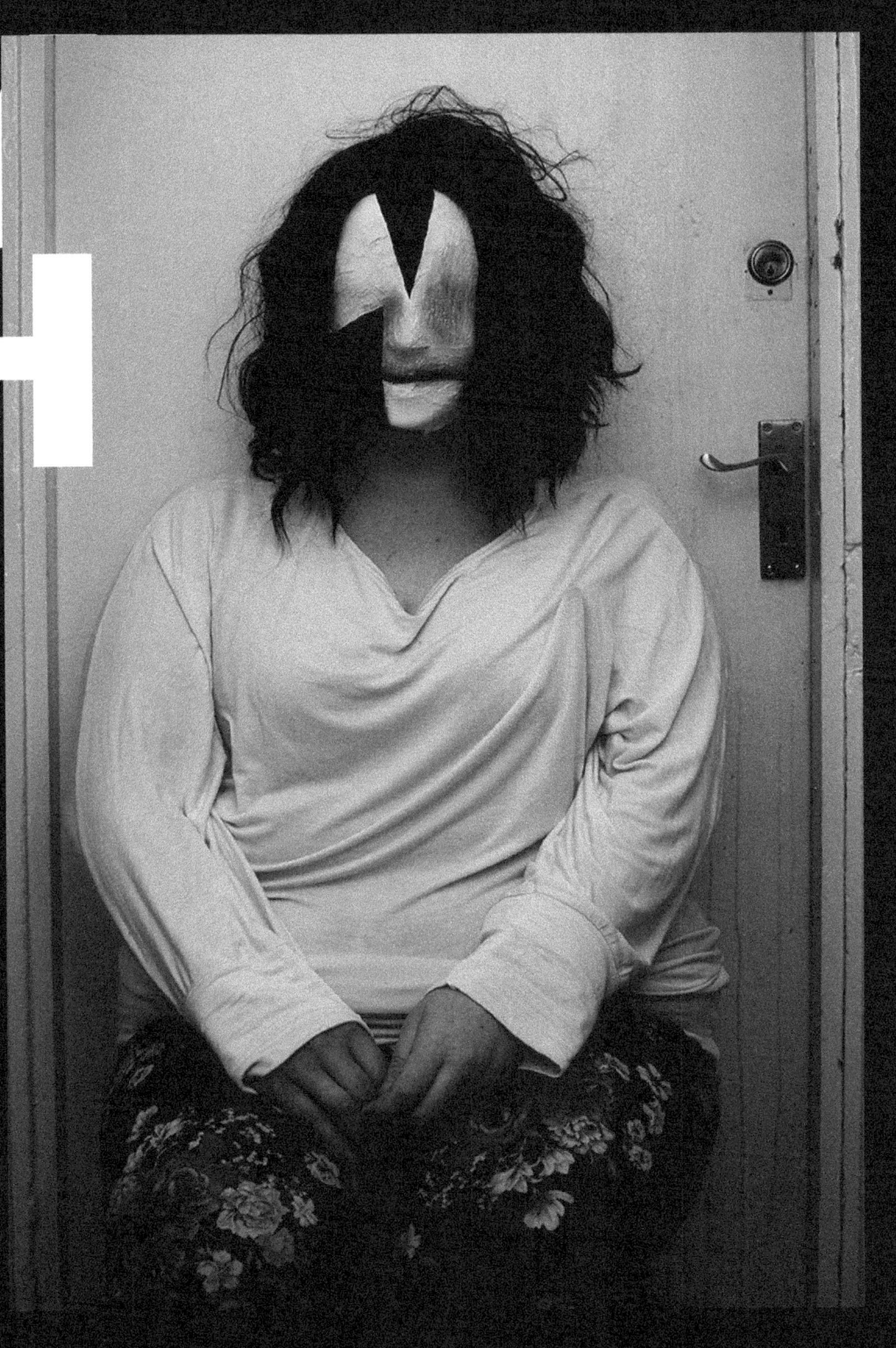

of Rosy Martin and Jo Spence who developed phototherapy in the 80's Nash also experiments with different methods of deconstruction and reconstruction of self portraits and other images in an attempt to draw content from the unconscious into the conscious as research into abstract expressionism which they would argue was a movement started by photographers and not the fine art painters. This is all practiced within the perimeters another of Nash's own written methodology of Auto- Pathography, developed from Freudian psychoanalytic theory which they wish to advance with a PhD.

Still life photography and night photography are among other genre's this artist's practice encompasses which are wonderful (sometimes frightening) tools to explore one's own unconscious. Jenny Nash identifies as non-binary placing them under the trans banner. But as they were assigned female at birth and only have relationships with men, they don't receive the homophobic abuse that others live with all their lives and will never face discrimination based on who they love. This artist feels this places them more in an LGBTQ+ ally position and that their photography is a tool they can use to fight stereotypes and strive for equality. Since 2018 this artist has taken part in 21 exhibitions in the UK and internationally has been featured in 14 magazines both physical and online and has had work published in 4 books. Nash was chosen for the Leyden Gallery Emerging Artist award and exhibition in 2020 for their development of Solo Phototherapy and Auto-Pathographial self portraiture practice. Their self portrait series "Sinnestäuschung" that re-enacted their visual hallucinations due to diagnosed Bipolar was shortlisted for the New Emergence Art Prize in 2021. Jenny's latest project is with Greenwich council developing photography workshops for young people with substance abuse issues to give the young people a way to communicate and express themselves, using photography as that interface that this artist discovered so long ago

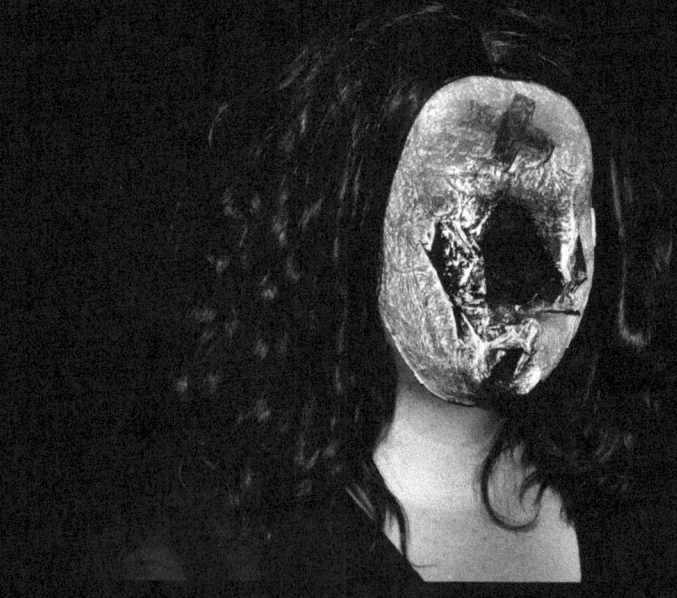

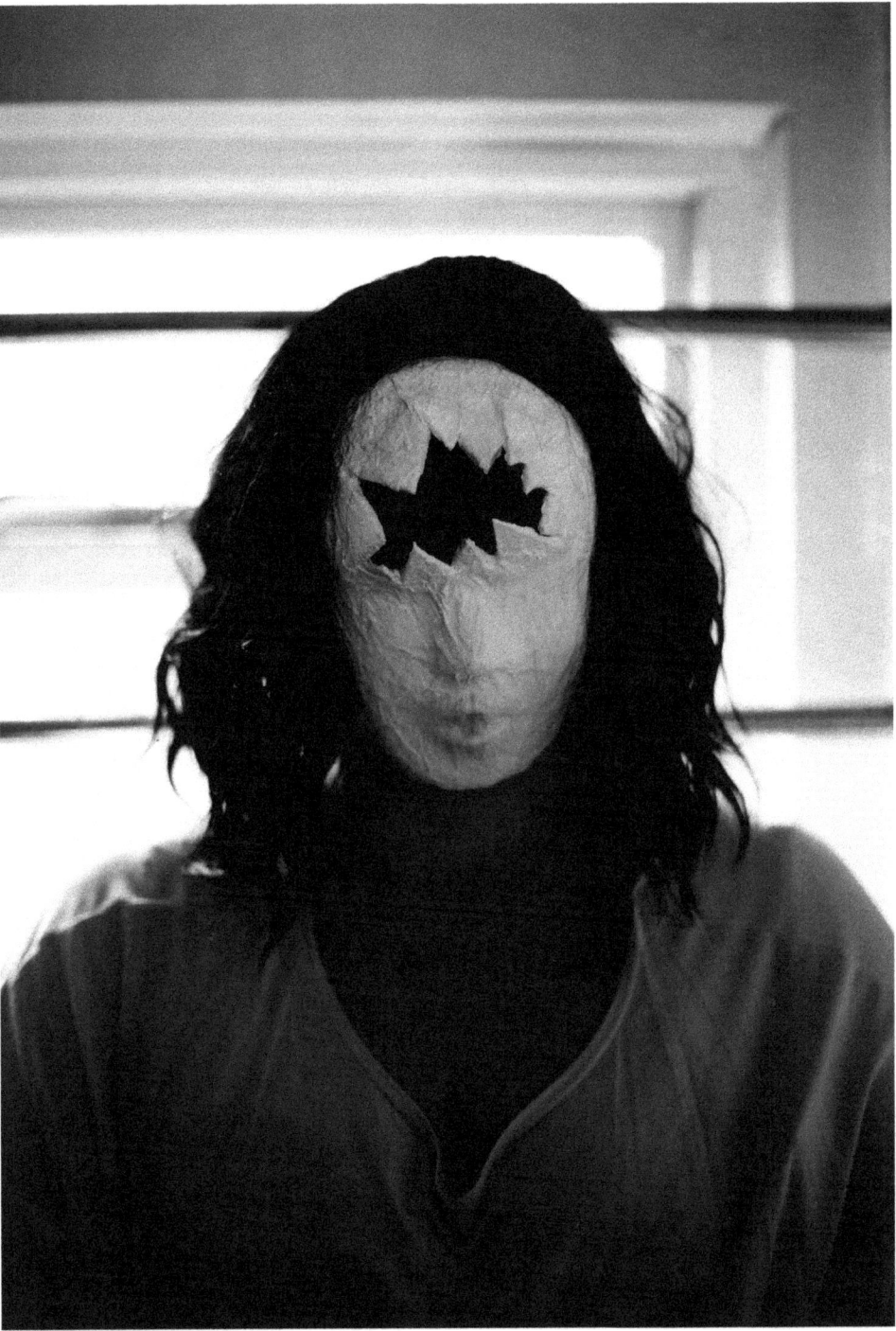

ISOLATION

Mid March 2020, I retreated into isolation aftercontracting the virus Covid-19. During this time the UK was put on lockdown by the government and online I observed recordings of the mad scramble of people trying to establish new forms of existing. The cracks in my country were beginning to show and some things fell through them.

The stockpiling of medication resulted in a 50% rise in demands for repeat prescriptions. The advice from the National Health Service to order prescriptions no more than ten days before needed, was not heeded. People's fear and uncertainty and, of course, selfishness, led to a vicious cycle of panic. The consequent strain on the NHS led to delays in restocking which predictably led to shortages.

I myself could not obtain the medication I take to manage bipolar disorder resulting in the experience of my own intense withdrawal symptoms over seven days.

Things are no longer as we once knew. Things once not thought about now require thought. We are all struggling with the loss of a world where things were going to be different and everyone will have a story to tell. However, my personal story is of imposed physical isolation and how I began to isolate internally. I depersonalised. The dark shadow emerged, a subversion of self that rendered me unsafe within the world I thought I knew.

In 1964 Ernst Becker states in relation to depersonalisation; "Rules, objects and self-feeling are fused, taken together they constitute one's 'world'. How is one to relinquish his world unless he first gains a new one. This is the basic problem of personality change."

Our personality is made up of our masks. Some we chose to wear, some we wear through necessity to survive. Some are inflicted on us. Anindividual doesn't always feel at the centre of their own personal world or that they have any ownership of it. This prevents them from being fully involved in living. Their development is caught between "The mirror and the mask". Caught between the analysis of others that reflects back a sense of their personal worth and a disguised search in which the self finds or seeks affirmation that they are enough, a reflection perhaps unseen by everyone.

These feelings of depersonalisation that washed over me during the week of withdrawal are symbolised here as 14 masks, 14 aspects of the isolated self. The period of withdrawal became a lucid dialogue with the faces that are usually held at bay. Seven of the darker aspects of my(self) at night goaded me upon the rooftop of my flat and I confronted them. Not the self looking back as an image in a mirror, but reflected upon as if looking into a mirror that might reflect my mind.

This project is dedicated to Daniel Furniss.

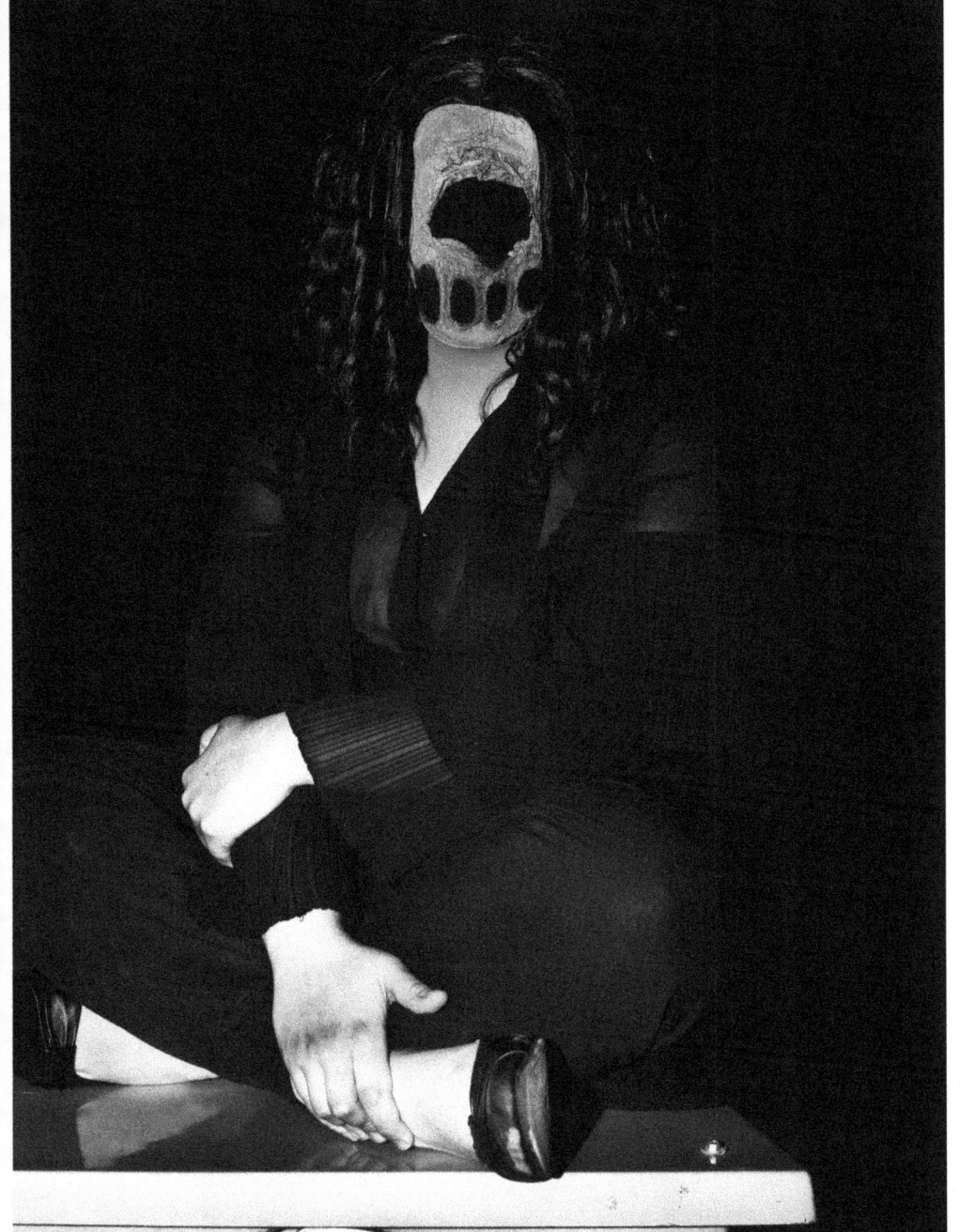

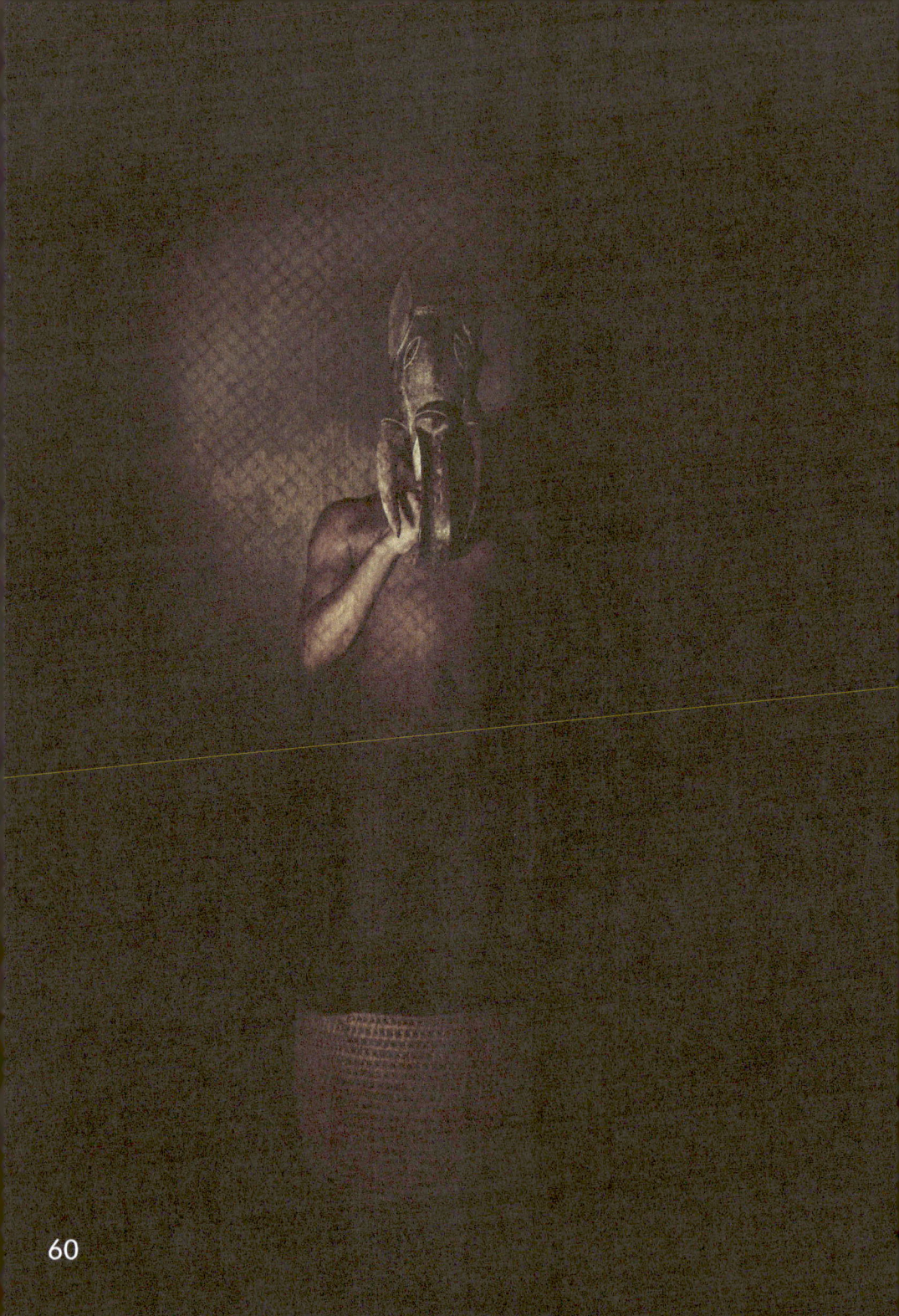

GIL MUALEM-DORON

Gil Mualem-Doron (1970 UK/Israel) is an award-wining socially and politically engaged artist working in various media; primarily photography, digital art, installation and performance using participatory practices. His work investigates issues such as urban history, social justice, identity, transcultural aesthetics, migrations and displacement.

www.gmdart.com
www. trianglein.org

THE ALIEN

A series of photos and a recorded conversation with Keith (pseudonym) – "an illegal" migrant that escapes persecution as a gay man in Malawi and moved to Cape Town, South Africa. Keith is an undocumented migrant with no rights and is facing deportation. The conversation with Keith that took place before the photo shoot is integral to the work and can be read here.

The series "Alien" is part of the socially engaged photography project "No Man's Lands".

No Man's Lands (2016-) is an ongoing art photography project that uses a collaborative approach to convey the stories of men that are or were in limbo circumstances due to political, social, economic, or other factors. On the surface, the portraits are of individual men, yet as a whole, they also reflect contemporary global issues such as political persecution, the effects of wars or economic inequality, racial discrimination, persecution of LGBT persons, and more. As part of his socially engaged art practice, the photoshoots are based on long conversation/s with photographs about their personal stories as well as on the ways they would like to be photographed and represent their story

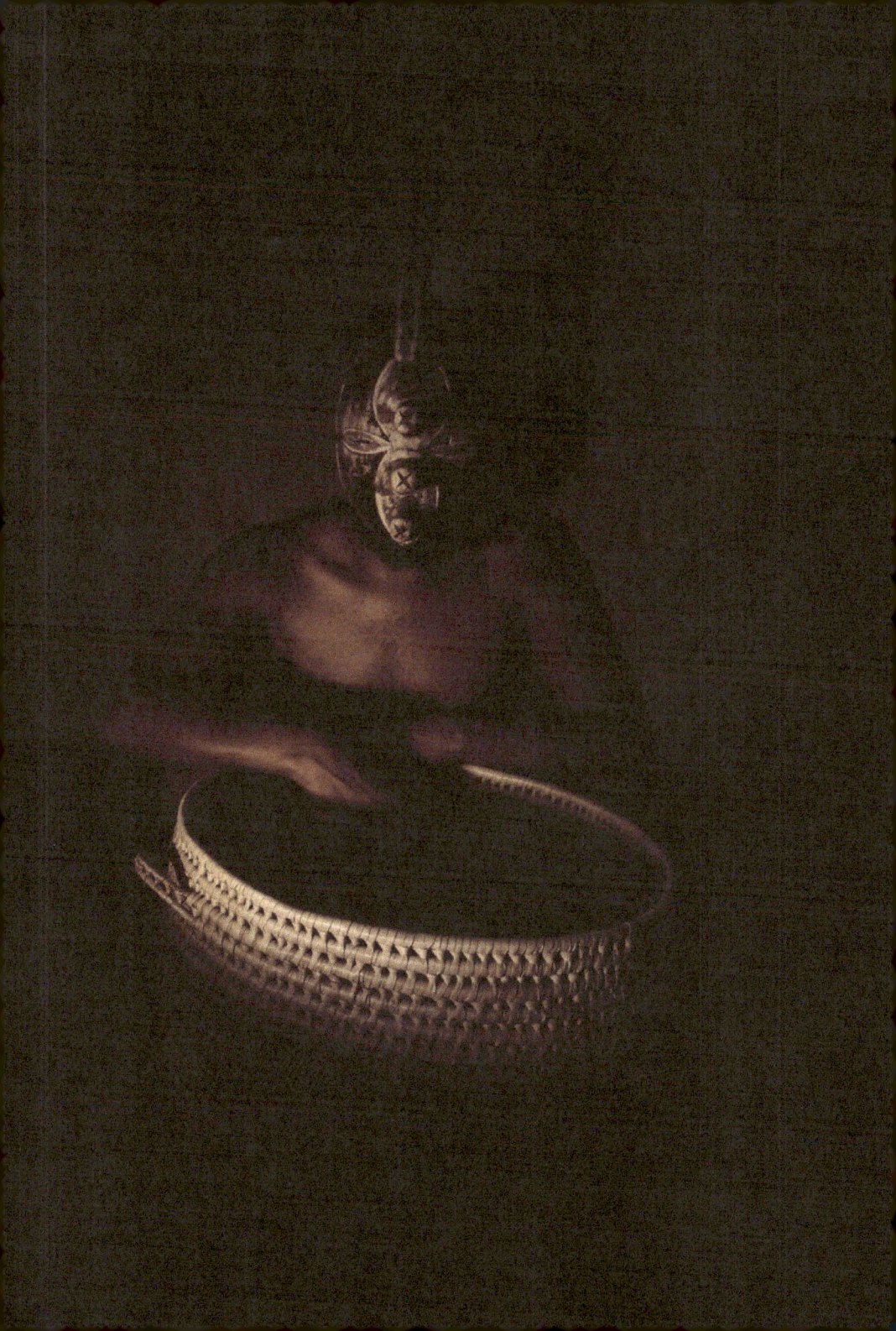

"Okay. Hi my name is Keith, I am originally from Malawi and 25 years old. I've been in Cape Town for 10 years now. Leaving home, it was like one of those decisions which one has to make so that you can be free somewhere, be yourself somewhere, and find a better life somewhere time to have some sort of damage to create. After I finished high school, I was on holiday with my friend who was helping with some home mathematics and geography because I was good at them. So we started hav

things like that in one of those days my mom came across us busy in bed and everything like that so she chase me from my house and I had to live with this guy for a certain time. After this guy he wrote his exam, he passed and his parents brought him to South Africa so that he could further his education. So he went to the University of UJ and then he wanted me to come this side as well so that is why I came to this side. So after I came to this side, things change, we didn't click that much and everything like that so I was like okay

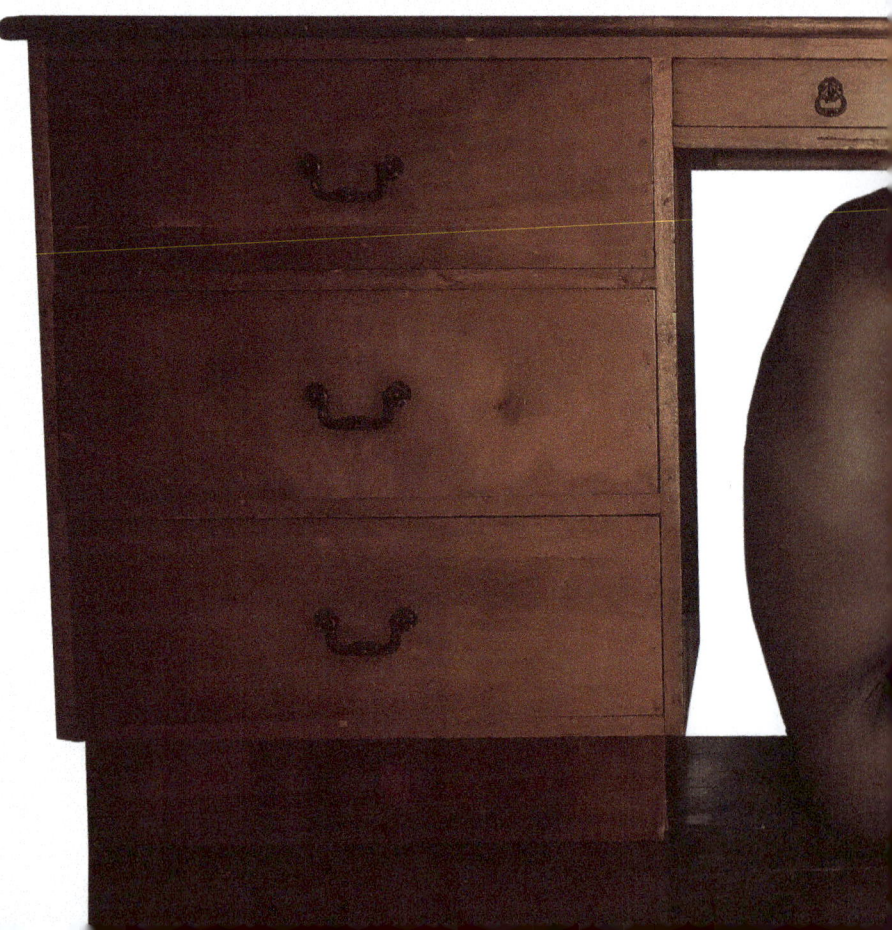

own life somewhere else and I left ____ to come to Cape Town because I had one of my friends living here. So I said living by myself from then until now.

Being in Cape Town, Cape Town life is so expensive, like it's very expensive for rental. And, to get a job is very difficult as well. And the time when I came in Cape Town, newcomers, like new refugees who were not allowed to get payments in Cape Town so we need to apply in ___, in ___, in Jo'berg, or in PE, so for the time being, at that time I was young, I couldn't get hired, and I couldn't get a proper job so that I can save up some money and go and apply for asylum and all of these ways that I have mentioned about. So up to now I'm still undocumented and I do get some paid jobs but it's hard to get a proper job because you are foreign and secondly, undocumented. So at the moment, I'm working so hard to get myself documented, to get myself a proper job, and possibly maybe study again further because I just did my high school and I didn't do

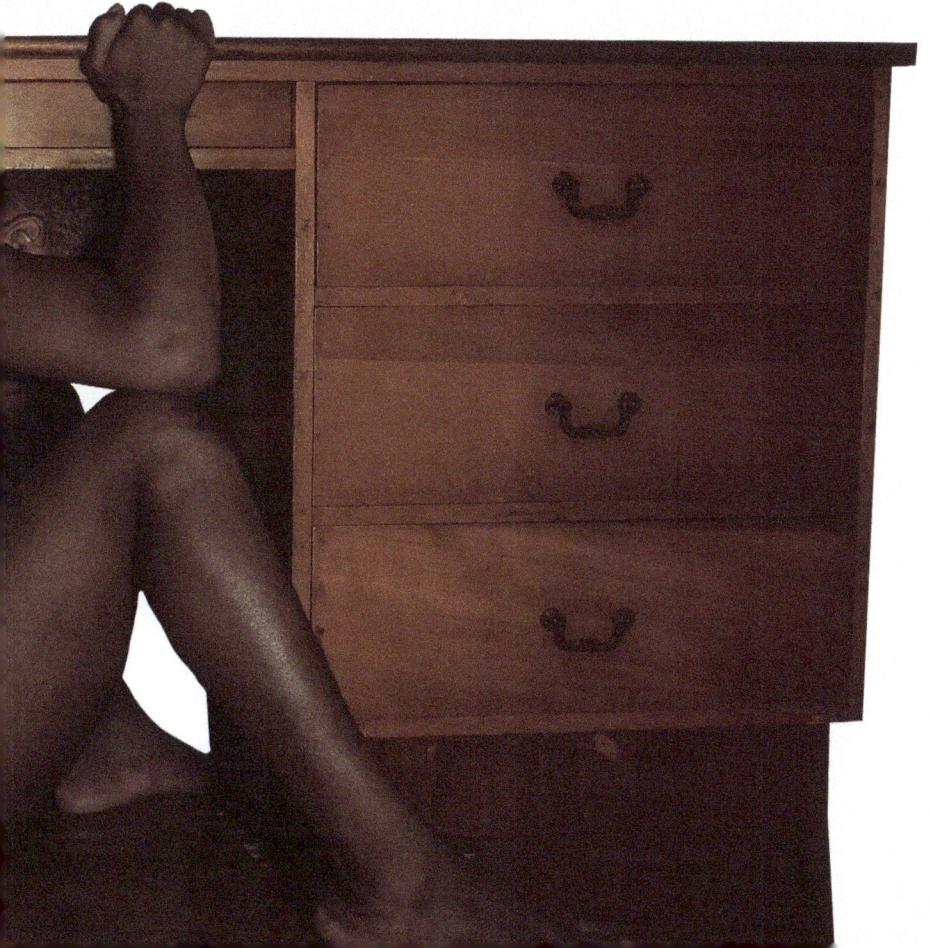

anything further. So life here is good because I'm free, I'm myself and like back home in Malawi, it's not gay-friendly.

Is it illegal?

It's illegal to be gay in Malawi and here I kind of find myself. There are people who are gay, who are L. G. B. T. Q. I. I feel like it's home and I'm not thinking about going home. So I'm working towards going back to school and having a better life of living here.

Do you know any of the gay people who came from other countries in Africa in which is not legal and got asylum in South Africa because of being gay?

Not everyone is lucky to get asylum. You can even go and apply for asylum but the reason you specify like specifying about being LGBTQ like there's some question they ask like 'how do you have sex? Prove to us that you are gay'. How can you prove to someone so that you can get asylum, so things like that, there are so many critical questions that they ask and then you end up failing to answer the appropriate answer. So there's not a

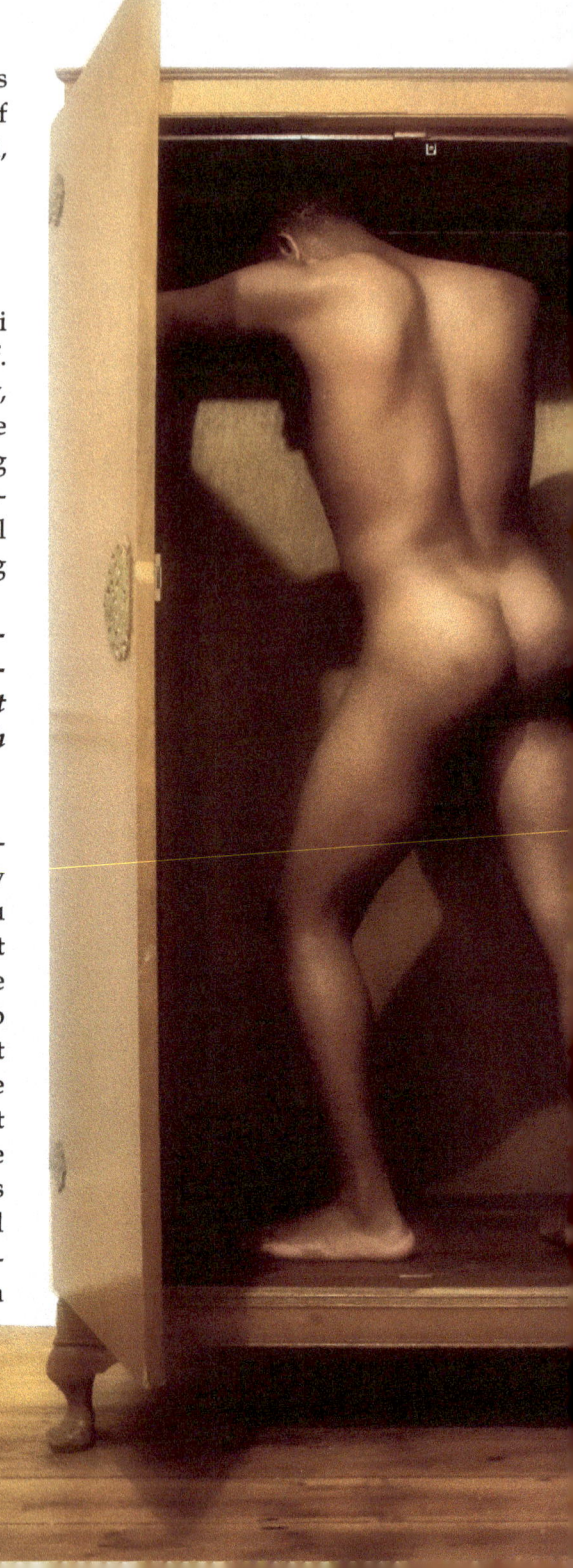

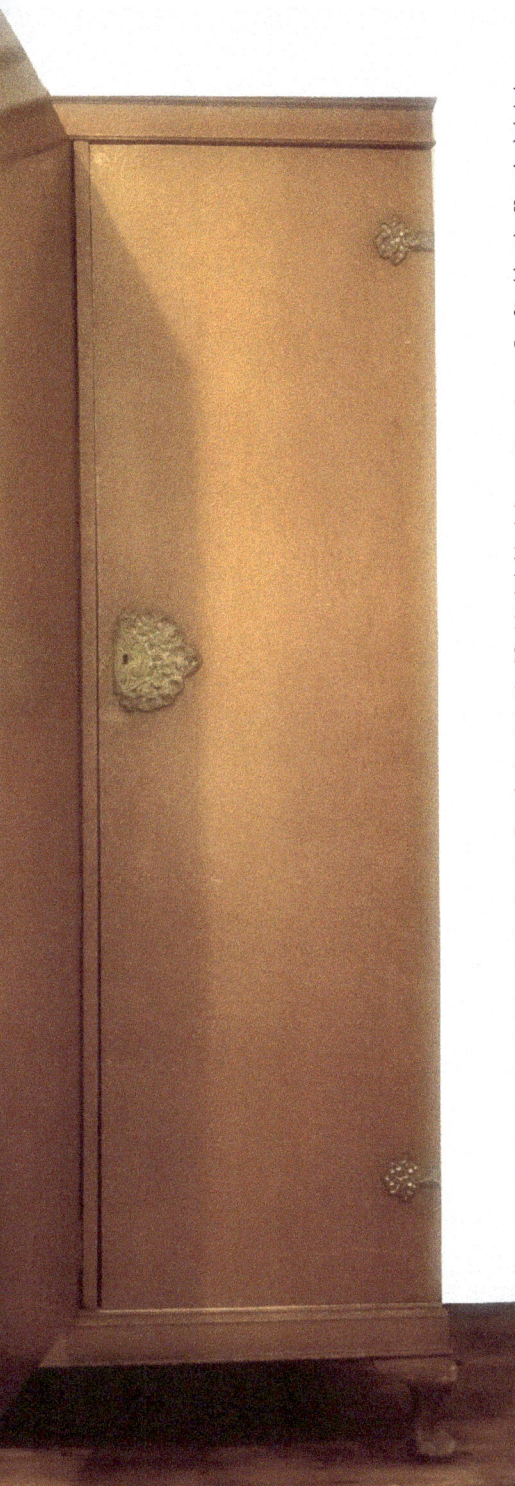

lot of people that I know that have and gain asylum because they do issue 1 but you go into so much screening and questioning for you to get one so it's not even easy for you to get an asylum based on your sexual orientation.

What do you need to prove to them?

I've got a trans woman who is from Uganda. She had to prove herself that she's trans by showing pictures of her as a man. Some of the questions which they were asking her were not like a gay guy or a trans woman and you probably know that you get sex through anal intercourse, you know, so those are the kind of questions that they do ask you. And if you're not comfortable talking about it or you're not free to talk about it, you're nervous talking about it or something like that, you end up having it canceled and not to get asylum or status or documentation and the legal paper to live in the country. So it's not as easy as everyone thinks to get it."

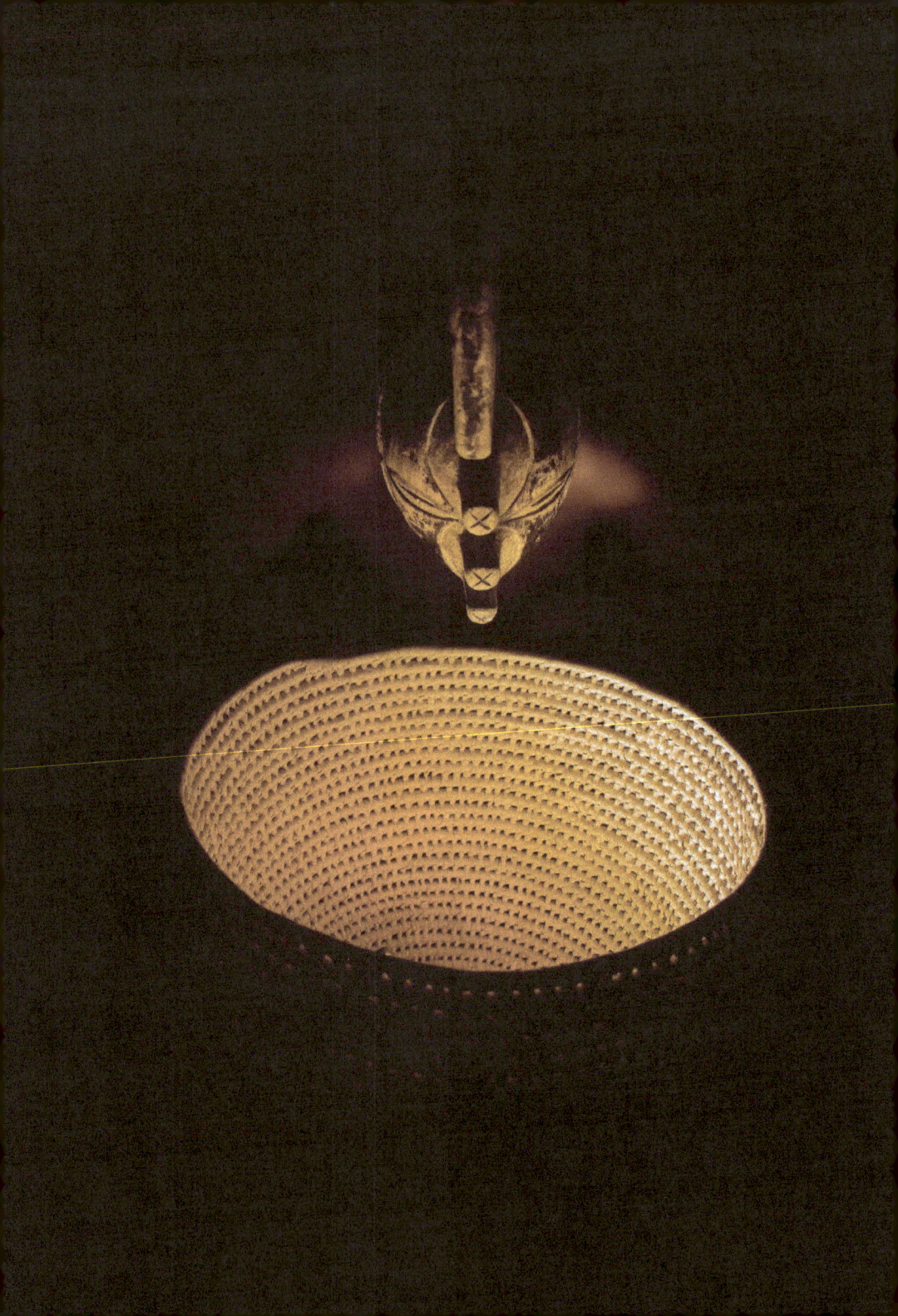

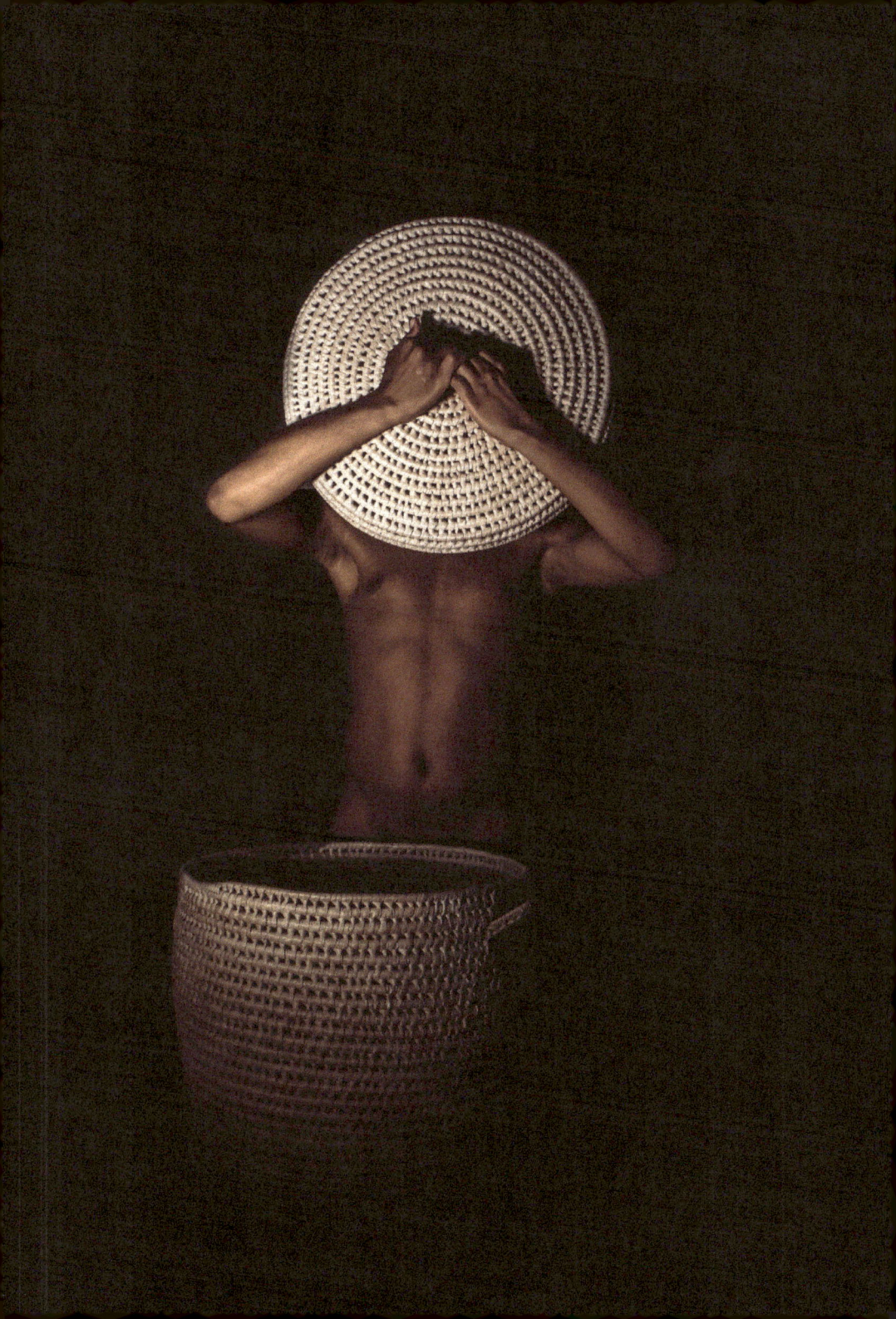

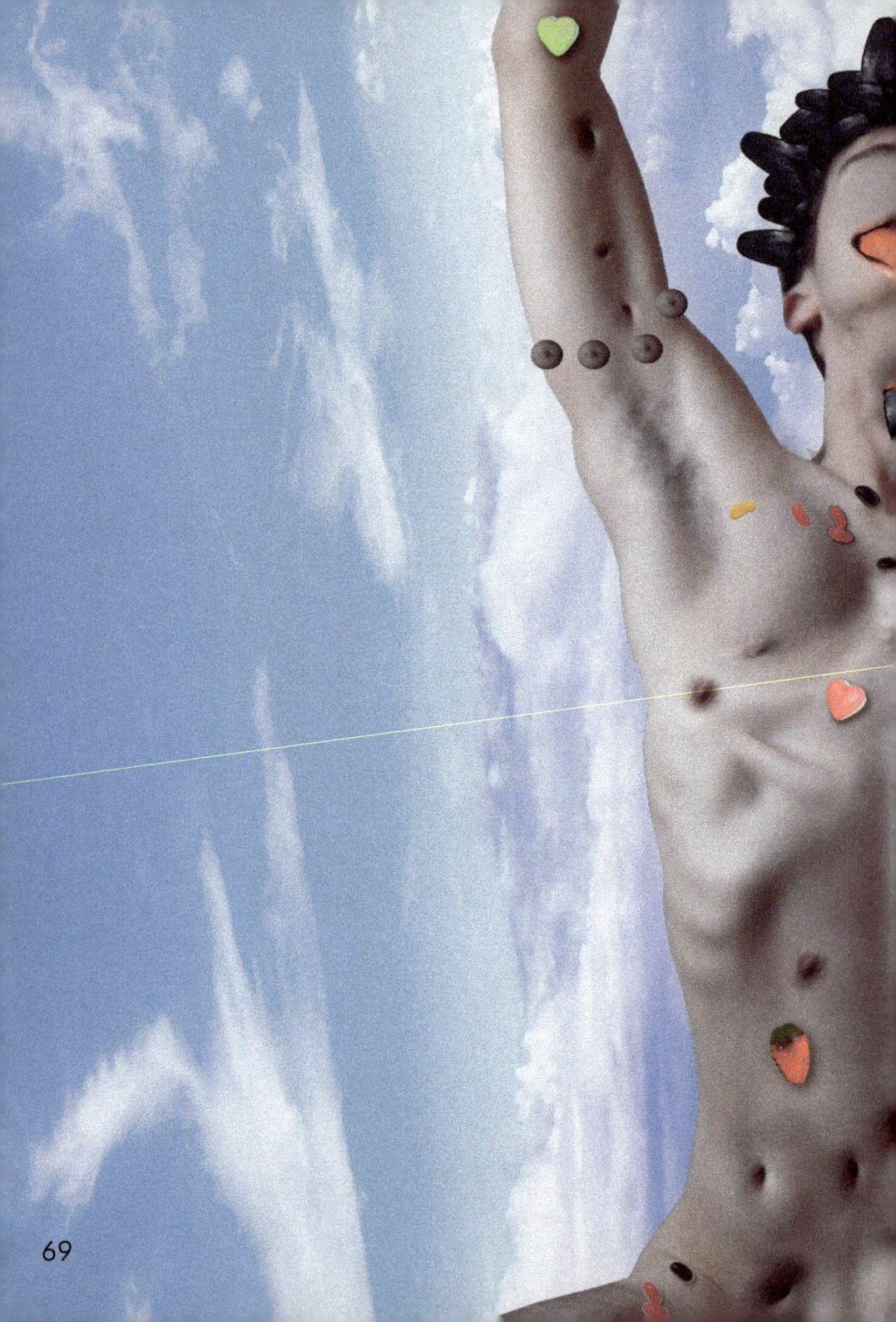

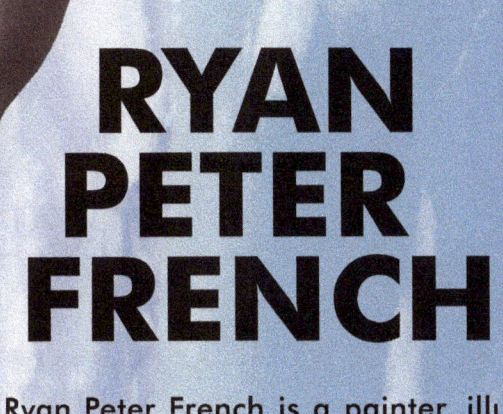

RYAN PETER FRENCH

Ryan Peter French is a painter, illustrator and digital media artist currently based in Manchester. The subject matter of his work lies in the human condition, the ability to share and connect our experiences through visual language, and the necessity of fantasy in the face of reality. French is currently exhibiting his digital works and illustrating the queer-horror graphic novel 'Love Bug'.

www.ryanpeterfrench.com
@ryanpeterfrench

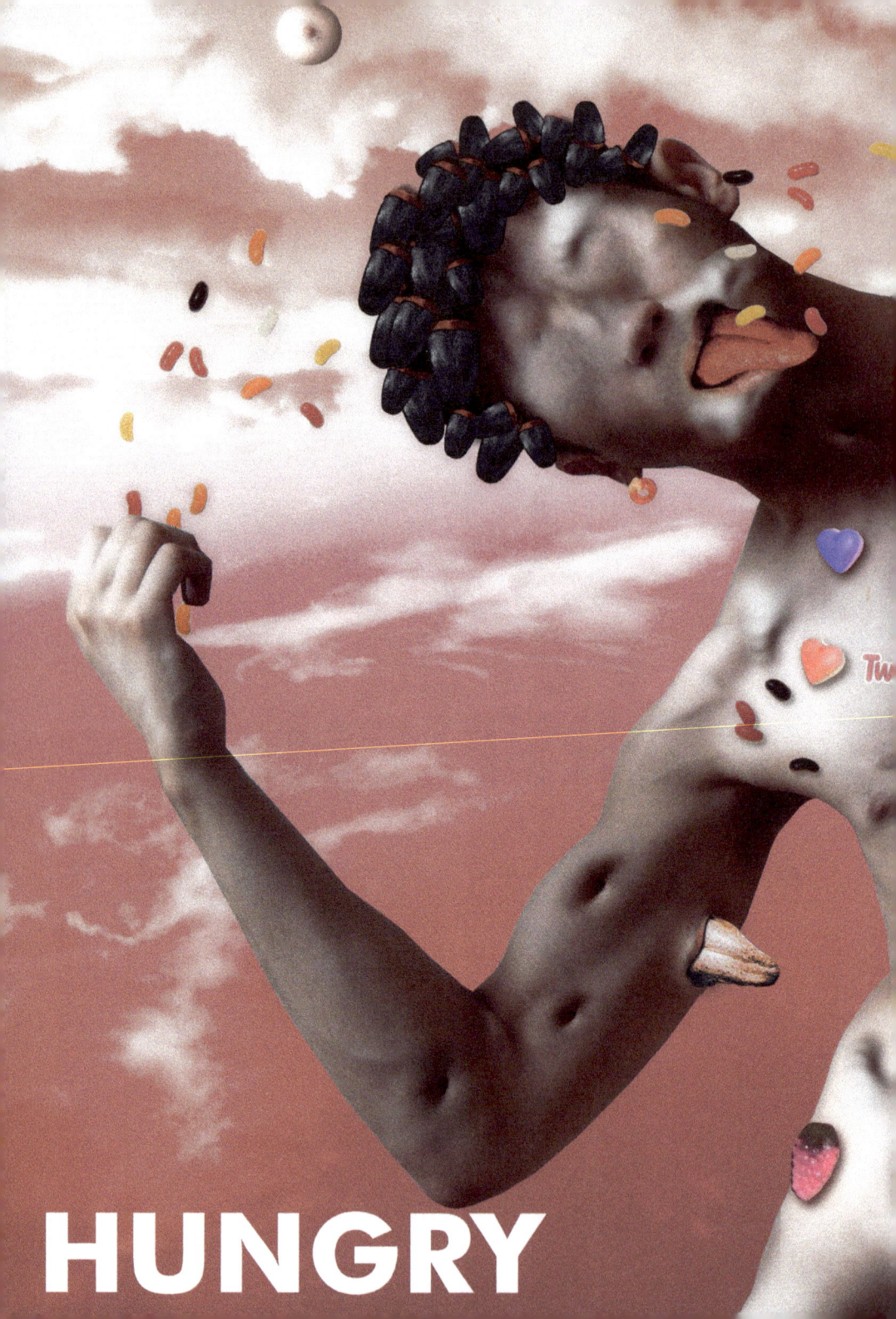

HUNGRY

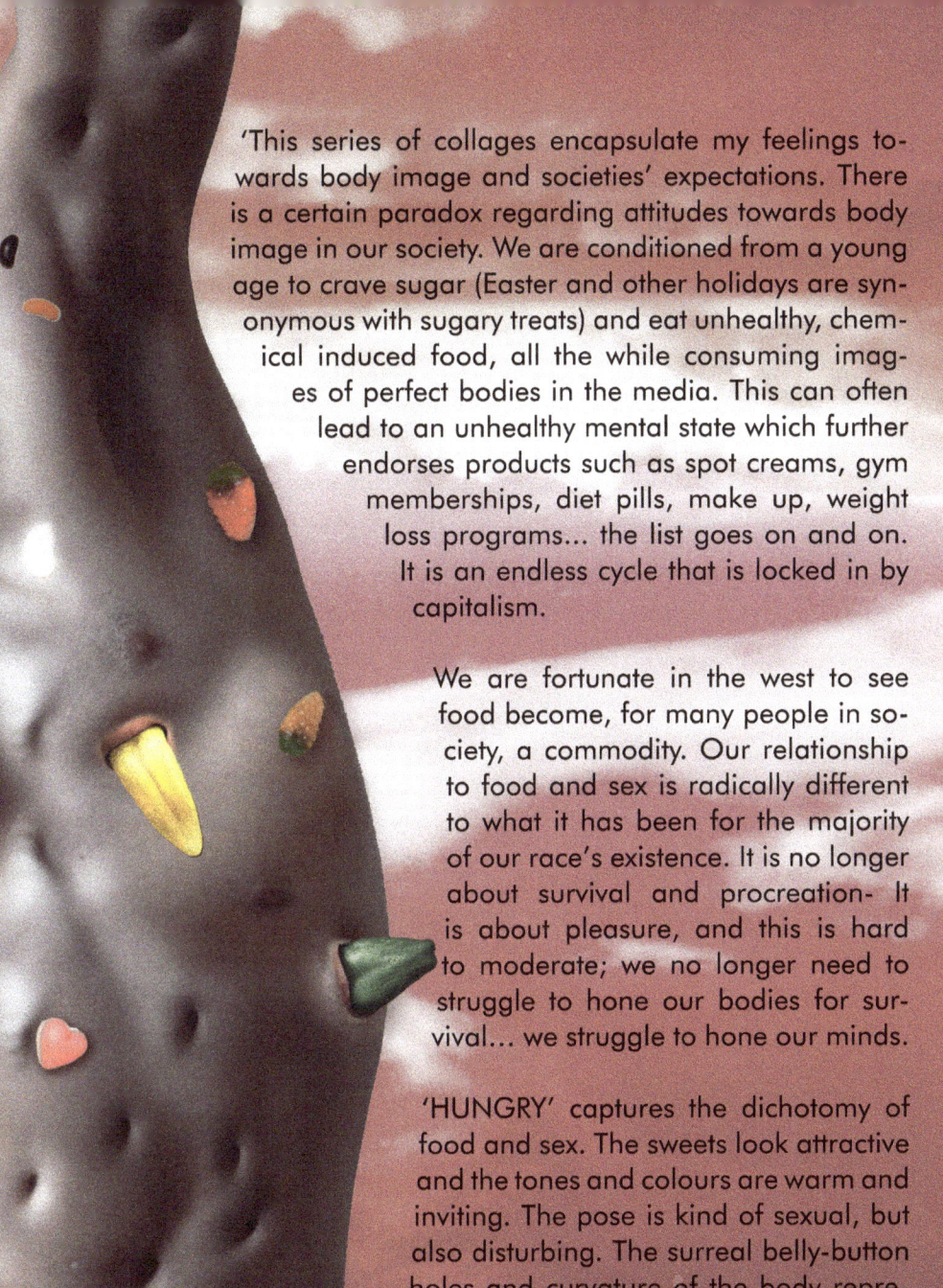

'This series of collages encapsulate my feelings towards body image and societies' expectations. There is a certain paradox regarding attitudes towards body image in our society. We are conditioned from a young age to crave sugar (Easter and other holidays are synonymous with sugary treats) and eat unhealthy, chemical induced food, all the while consuming images of perfect bodies in the media. This can often lead to an unhealthy mental state which further endorses products such as spot creams, gym memberships, diet pills, make up, weight loss programs... the list goes on and on. It is an endless cycle that is locked in by capitalism.

We are fortunate in the west to see food become, for many people in society, a commodity. Our relationship to food and sex is radically different to what it has been for the majority of our race's existence. It is no longer about survival and procreation- It is about pleasure, and this is hard to moderate; we no longer need to struggle to hone our bodies for survival... we struggle to hone our minds.

'HUNGRY' captures the dichotomy of food and sex. The sweets look attractive and the tones and colours are warm and inviting. The pose is kind of sexual, but also disturbing. The surreal belly-button holes and curvature of the body represent dysmorphia, and the tongues the ever insatiable hunger for pleasure.'

Beth Easton is a queer, nonbinary trans illustrator, and comic artist. Their work has been published in Boshemia (@boshemiamag), Sassify (@sassifyzine), and they are a regular contributor to The Happy 'Hood (@thehappyhood). Additionally Beth designs merch for the podcast Gender Reveal (@gendereveal). Beth's work was featured in the Mus um of Transology online residency in 2019. They host an online queer sketchbook club every two weeks to cultivate a safe community space for LGBTQ+ people. Beth uses they/them pronouns.

Visibility without rights, safety, education, and liberation means nothing. Making trans people more visible without creating a world where we are protected and allowed to thrive only sets us up for har-   assment   and harm.

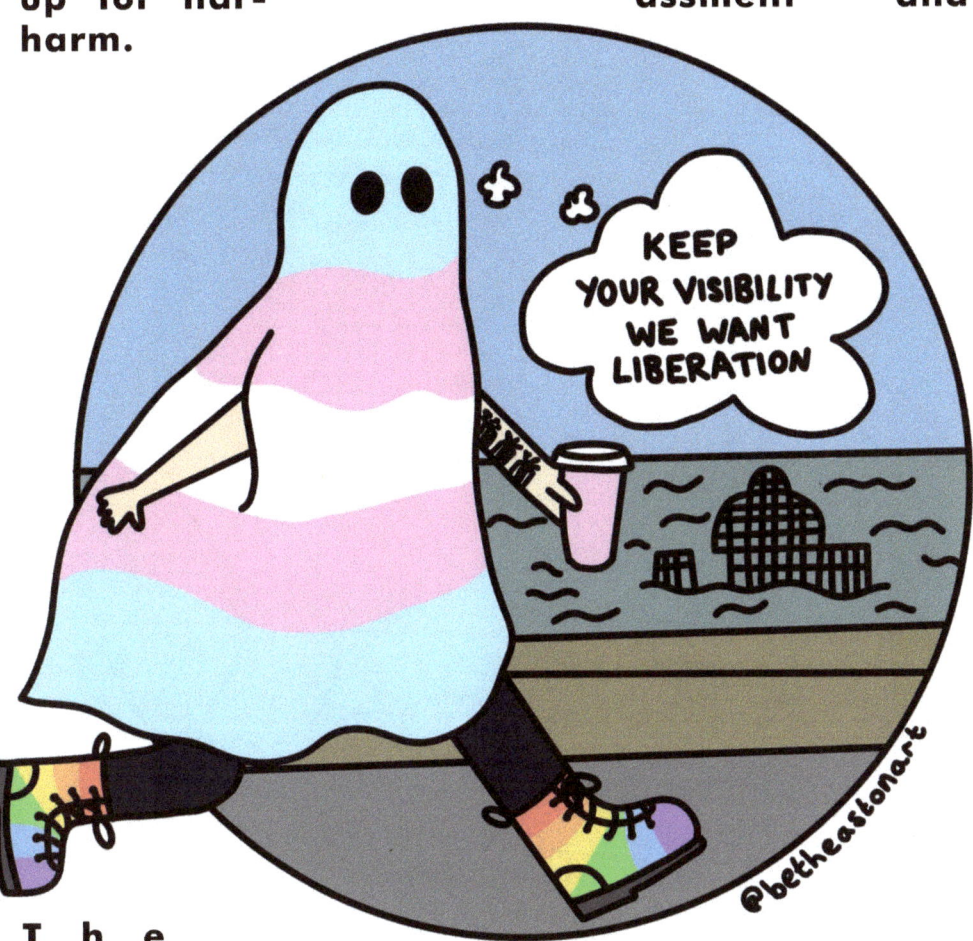

T h e problem   isn't lack of visibility,   the   problem is our systemic oppression, the direct attacks on our rights and healthcare, and the prioritising of cis people's opinions over our own lived experiences. Keep your visibility we want liberation.

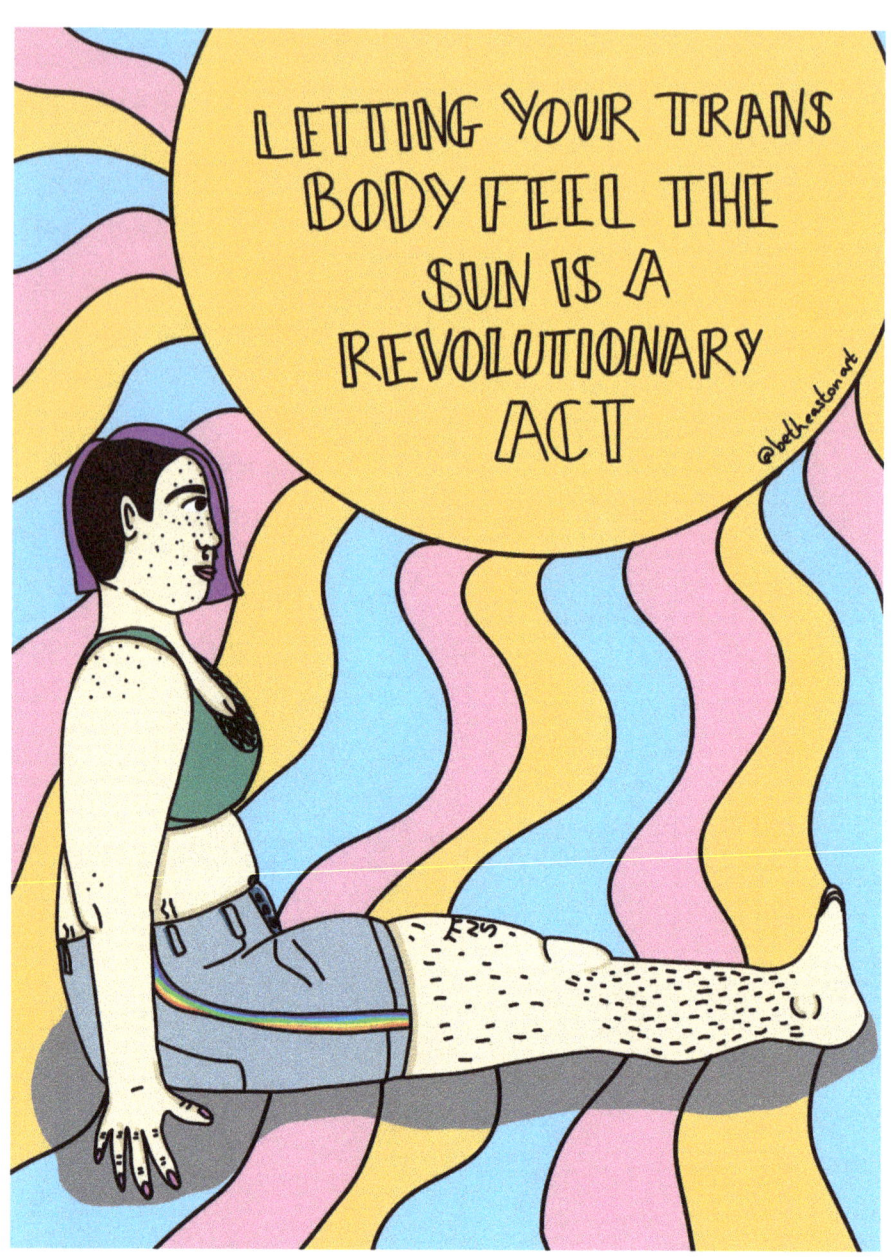

I know it's hard to enjoy the sun when you're full of dysphoria, but your trans body deserves to feel the sun. You deserve to enjoy it. Your body is magical and powerful.

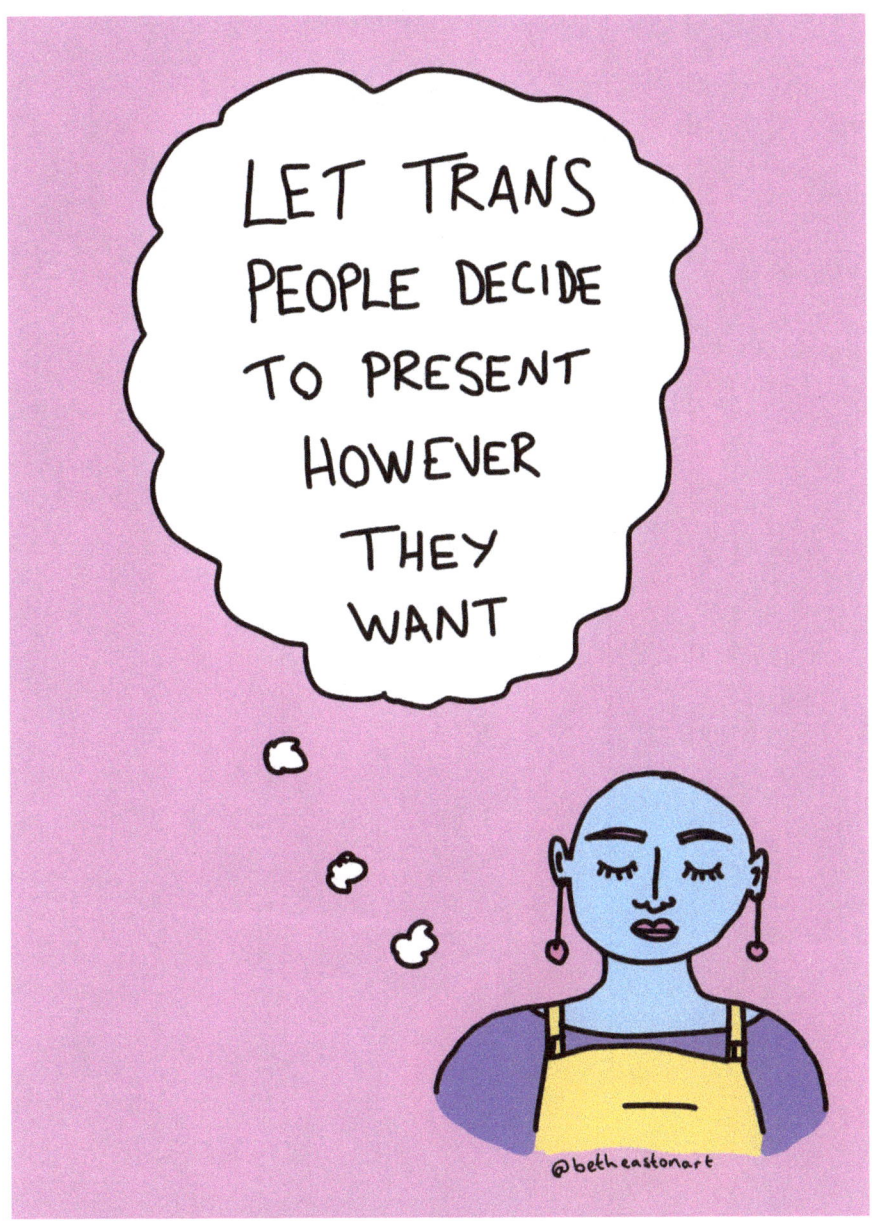

Trans bodies all look different and are all valid. All trans people are trans enough. There is no wrong way to be trans.

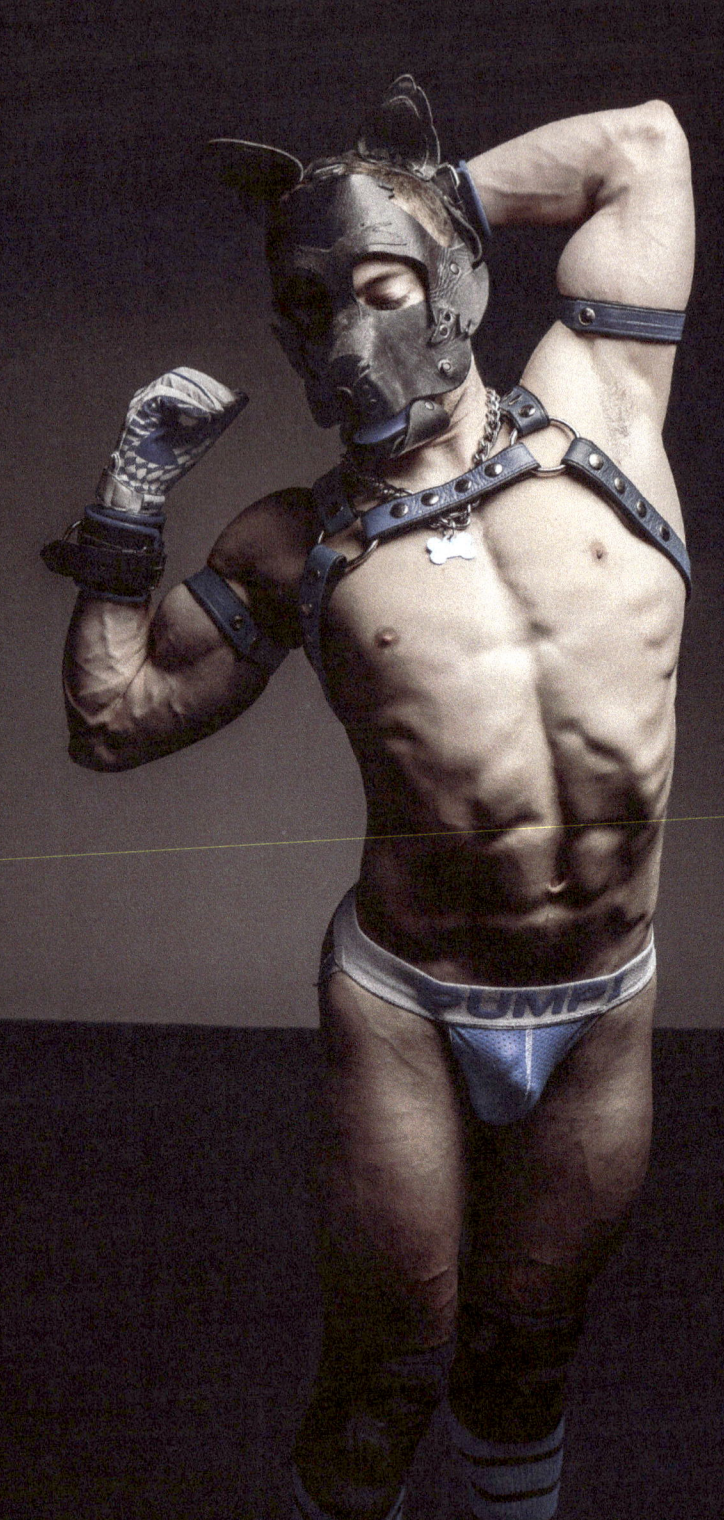

KEITH RACE-PUP

This series of photographs depicts a man engaged in pup play. Pet play is a fetish subculture within the wide world of BDSM (Bondage, Domination, Sad-Masochism) that exists in both the hetero and homsexual spheres of sexual expression via animal roleplay. Pup play began as a themed style of slave play where an individual would be 'degraded' for sexual satisfaction (of either or both parties). This would be achieved through a handler/pet relationship where a handler would treat their submissive just like a dog: forcing them to remain on all fours, eating via a dog bowl, and even stripping them of their human name. Pup play exists alongside pony play, kitty play and pig play among others.

Inspired by jamesnewland.co.uk

As the 80s punk culture took the world by storm, street fashion introduced leather, rubber and dog collars as common fashion on the streets and allowed for mainstream exposure of alternative culture on the TV and in music videos. With the ubiquity of internet access, images, videos and meetup sites dedicated to pup play moved online making it more accessible and normalised than ever.

Keith Race is a Canadian photographer and multidisciplinary artist-journalist who studied at Emily Carr Institute for Art and Design as well at Concordia University. His work has been published in VICE Magazine and the Washington Post, among others. He lives in Montreal where he runs a small photo studio in the heart of the gay village.

www.keithracephoto.com
info@keithracephoto.com
@SpacePupSilver

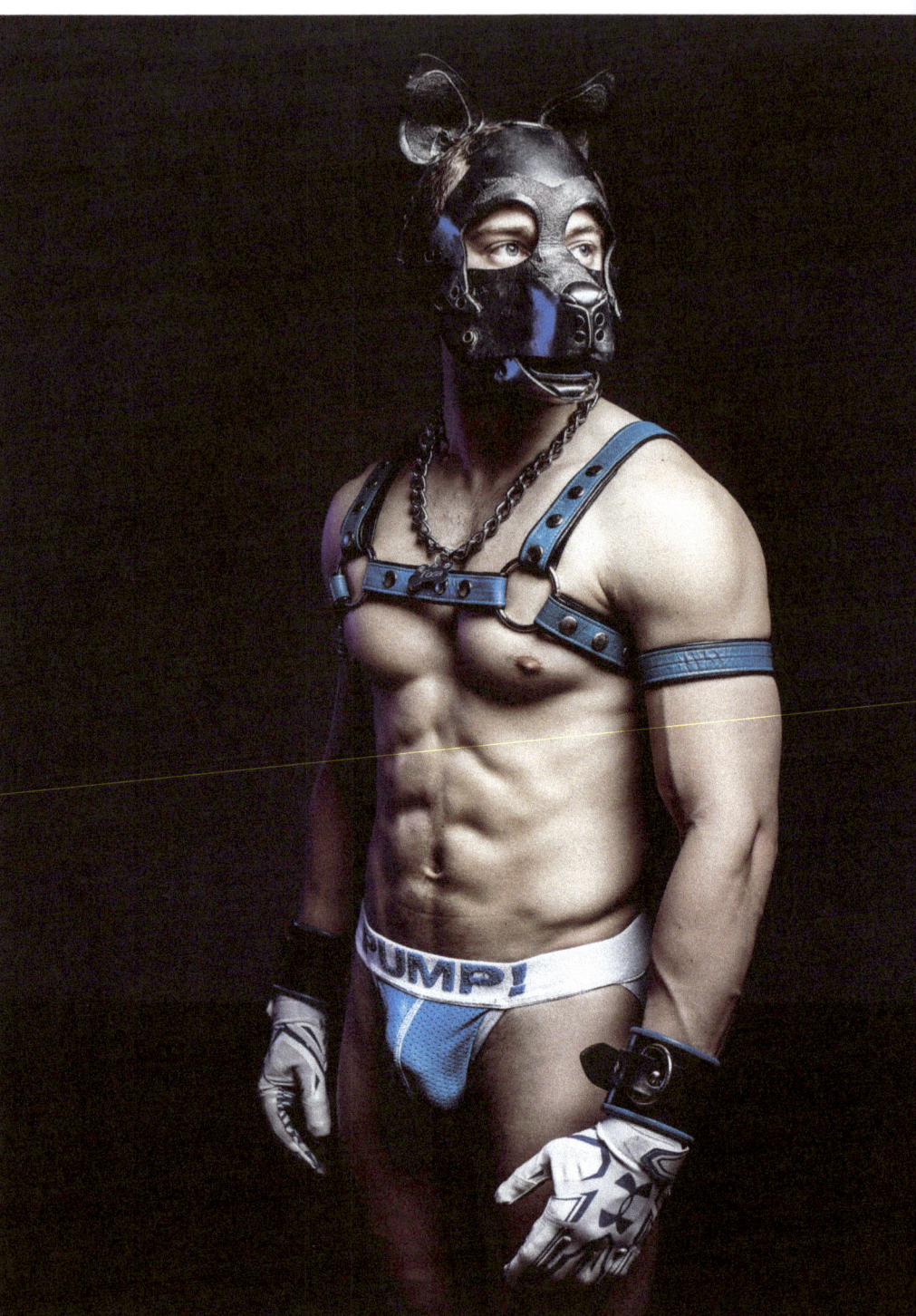

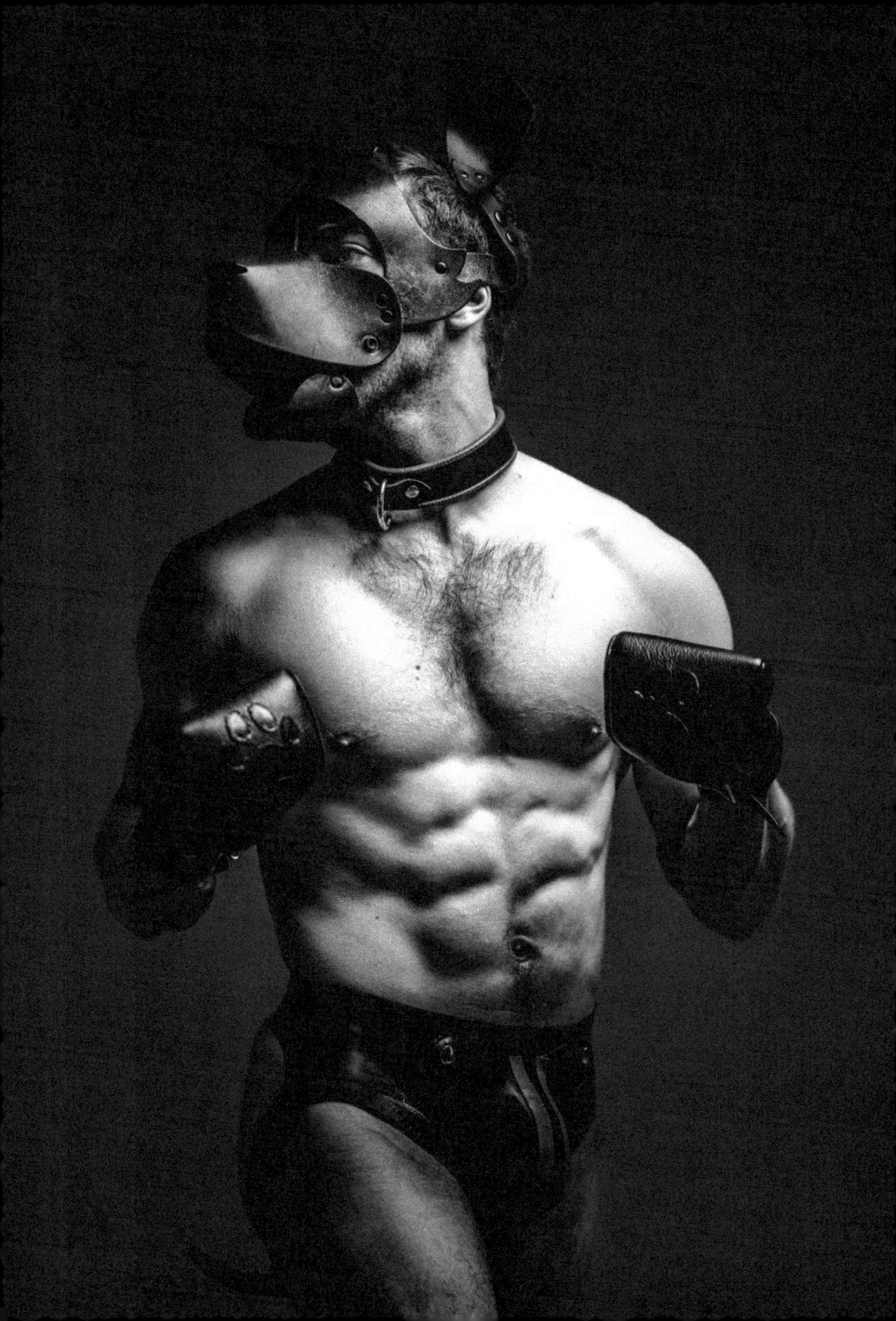

From the beefy gods of ancient times to the modern depiction of man's best friend, dogs have played a massive role in human culture. The zine gives a brief history covering the topic of "Human Puppies".

Pet play is a fetish subculture within the wide world of BDSM (Bondage, Domination, Sado-Masochism) that exists both in the Hetero and Homosexual spheres of sexual expression via animal roleplay.

Pup play (also called dog play) began as a themed style of slave play where and individual would be 'degraded' for sexual gratification. This would be achieved through a handler/pet relationship where a handler would treat their submissive just like a dog: forcing them to remain on all fours: eating via a dog bowl; and even stripping them of their human name to cement into the psyche that when in this 'headspace', they were not human and would not think as human.

Over the years, pet play has developed beyond its original roots into and act of fetish expression, beyond a simple dominant/submissive relationship. Pup play and Pony play are two majot categories within the culture but many alternative styles exist such as Kitty play and pig play.

Taken from: A Brief History of Puppy Play

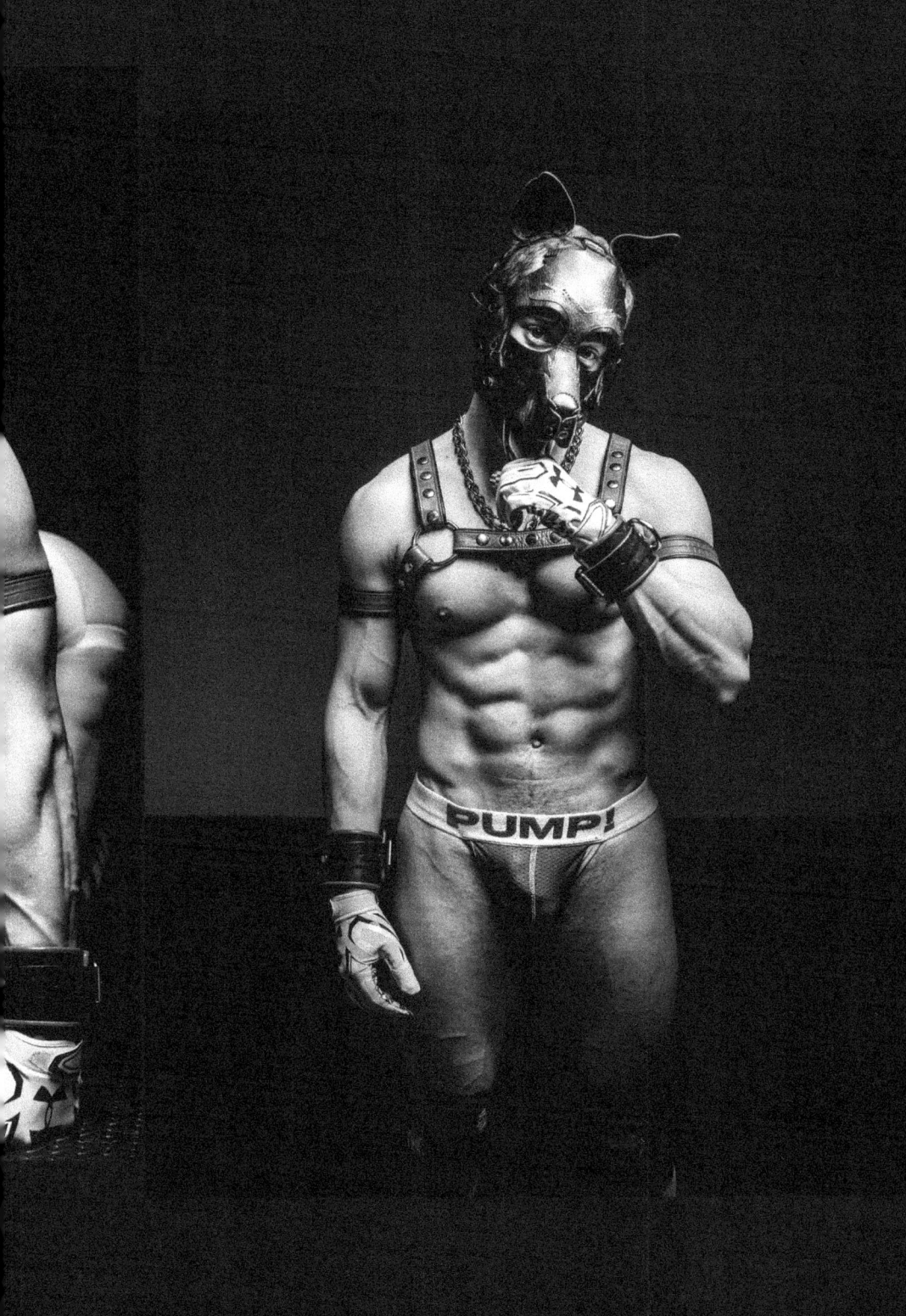

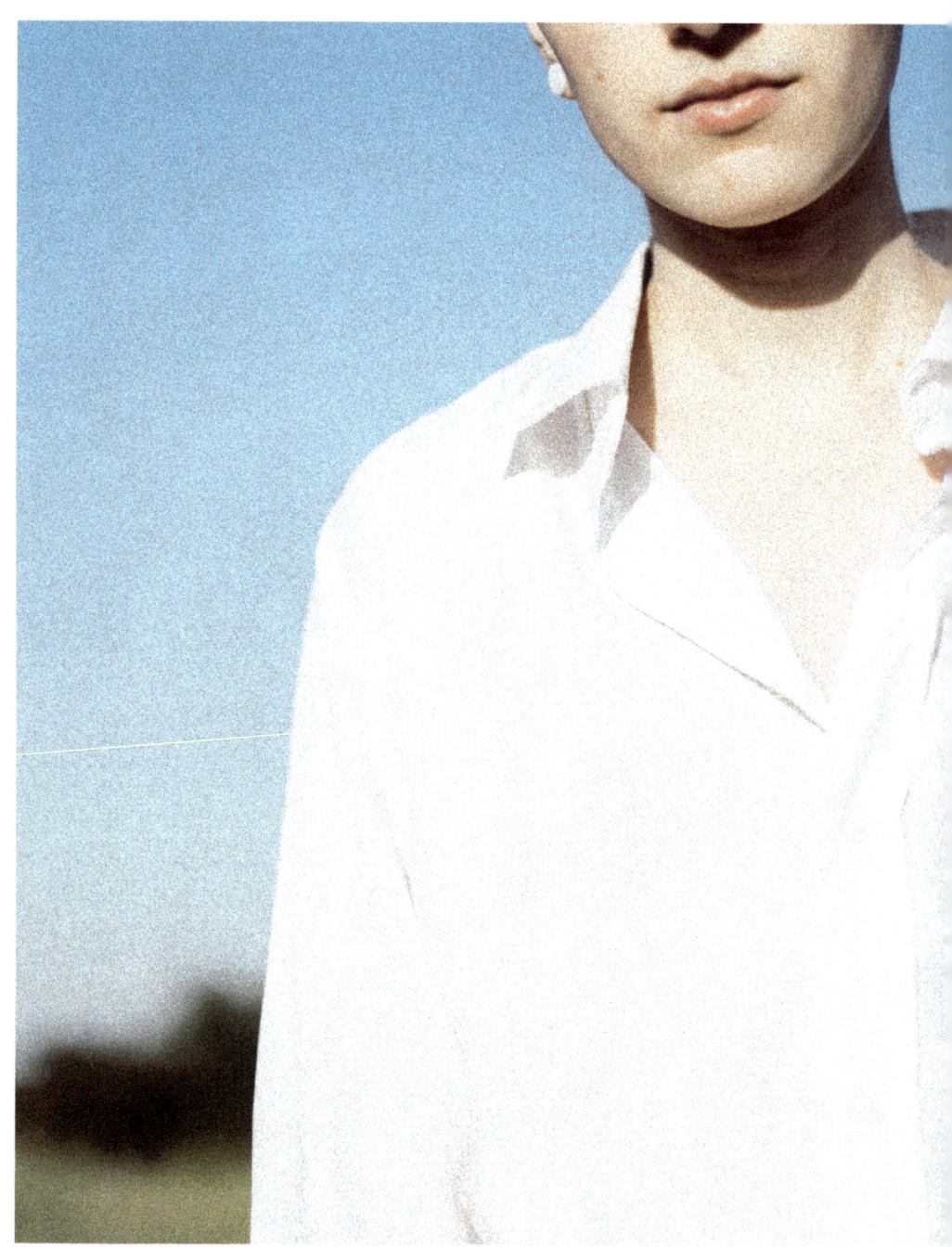

CONSTANZA
MIRANDA

I explore the relationship between body, intimacy, physical spaces and loneliness. Since the beginning of 2012 and up to the present, I had been researching a documentary group and foundation (www.mafi.tv). In 2015, I was part of a residence for artists in a rural commune of the country organised by the Government doing a photographic project trying to rescue the local identity through the active participation of the community. In 2016 I was selected along with 100 emerging artists from the country to participate in the FAXXI visual arts fair. During 2018 I made 3 exhibitions in the UK. Manchester - Leeds and the Liverpool Art Fair and I hope to expand my career to different places in the world. 2019, 2020 and 2021 I showed my work in Chile, the USA and UK in group exhibitions.

www.constanzamiranda.io

@cotidad

THE TRANSITION FROM JOSEPHINE TO JOSE, *A LUMINOUS PROCESS*

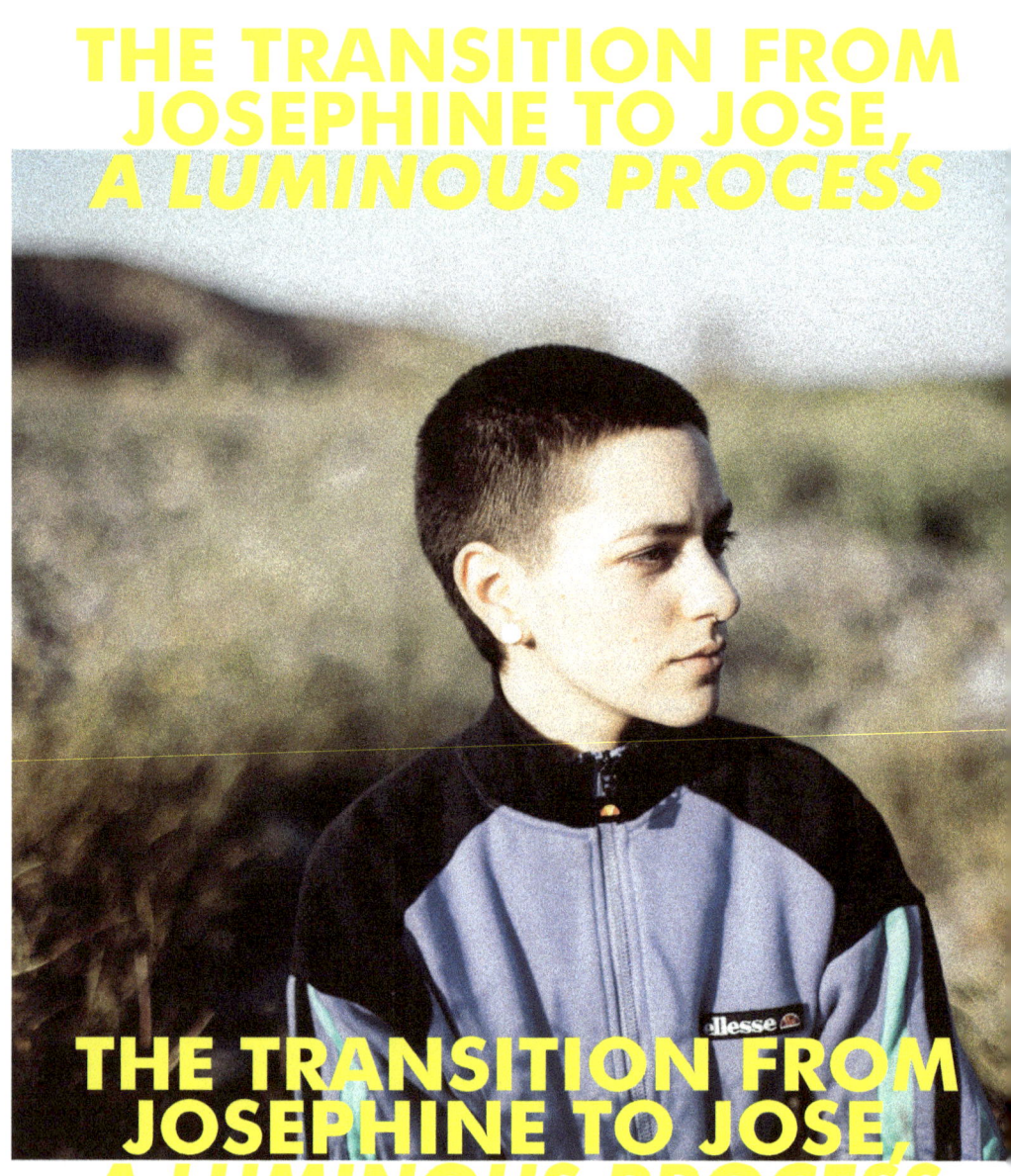

THE TRANSITION FROM JOSEPHINE TO JOSE, *A LUMINOUS PROCESS*

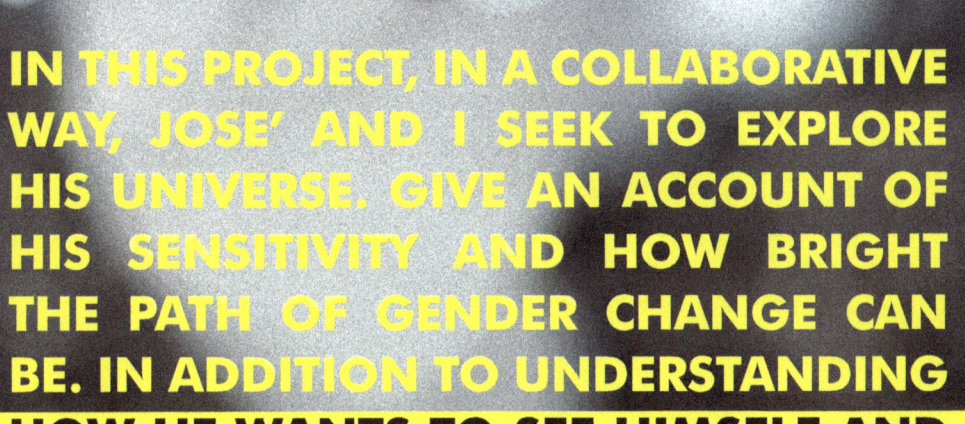

IN THIS PROJECT, IN A COLLABORATIVE WAY, JOSE' AND I SEEK TO EXPLORE HIS UNIVERSE. GIVE AN ACCOUNT OF HIS SENSITIVITY AND HOW BRIGHT THE PATH OF GENDER CHANGE CAN BE. IN ADDITION TO UNDERSTANDING HOW HE WANTS TO SEE HIMSELF AND SHOW HIMSELF IN FRONT OF THE REST. INHABITING THEIR SPACES AND RECOGNIZING THEM IN VISUAL TERMS ALLOWS US TO BE PART OF THIS JOURNEY THAT IS EXPRESSED IN THEIR WAY OF BEING-IN-THE-WORLD.

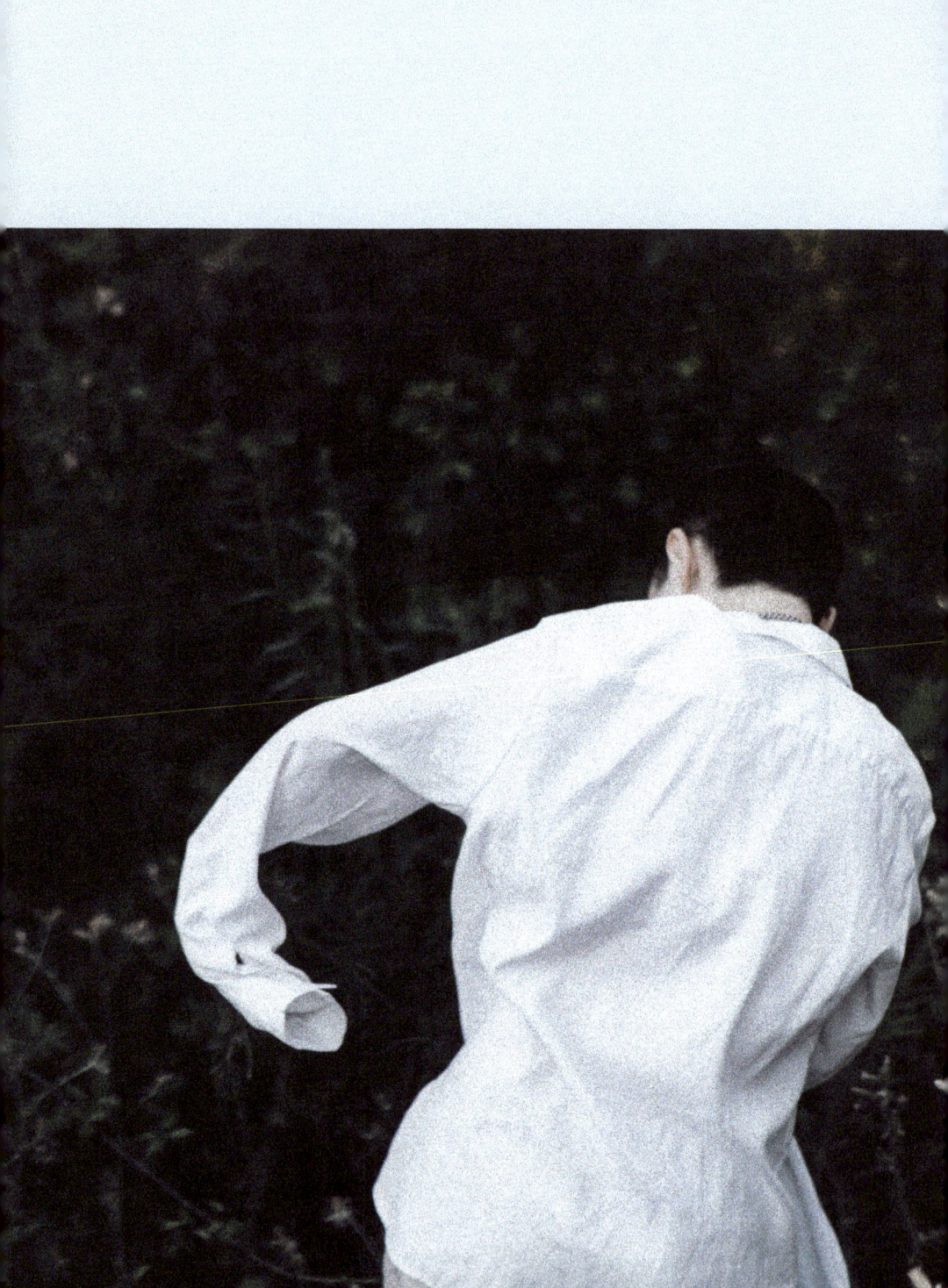

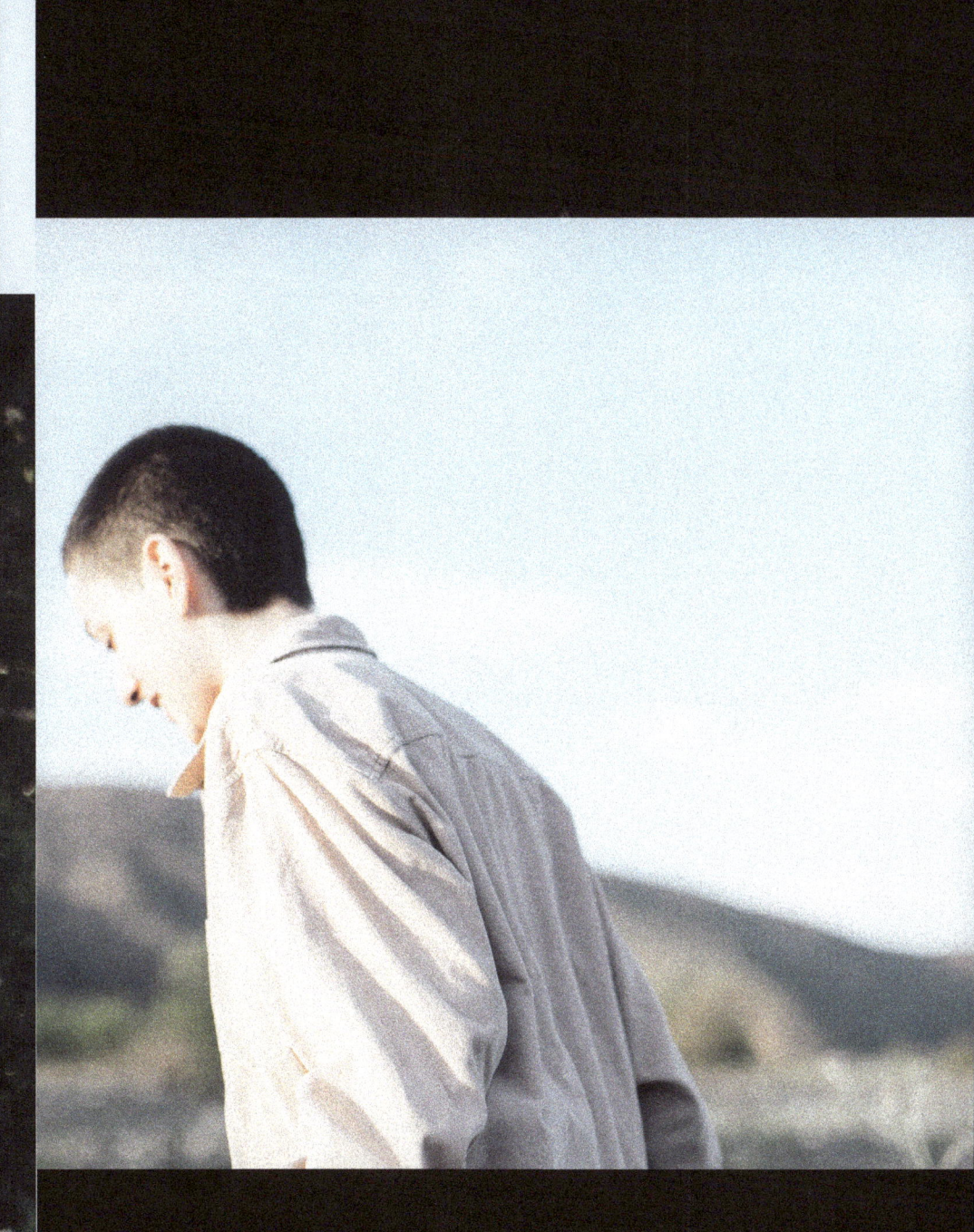

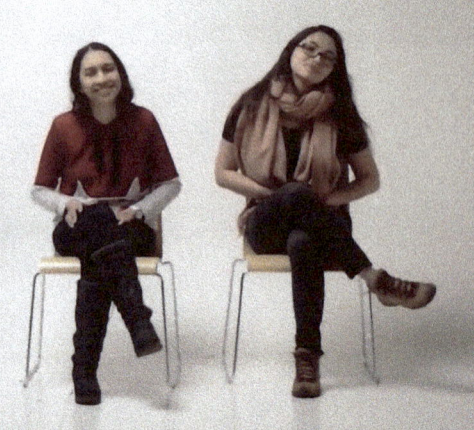
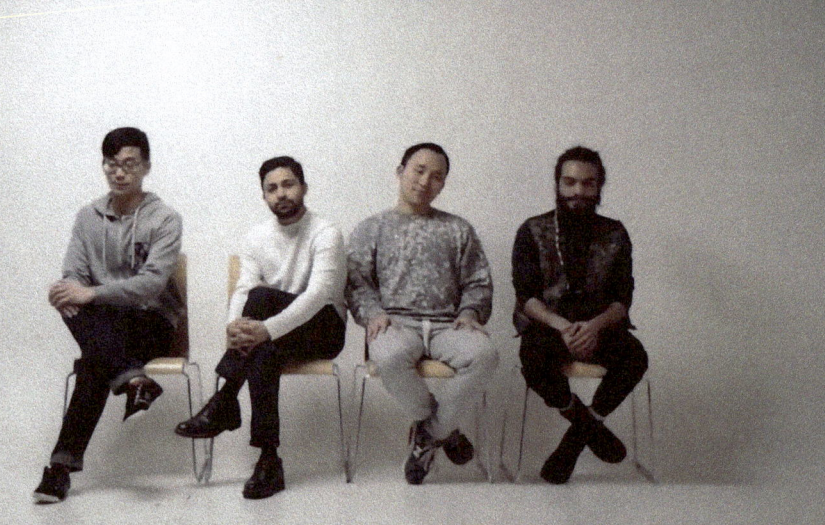

AUBANE BERTHOMMÉ MARTINEZ

Aubane Berthommé Martinez is an artist, curator, and a million of other things. Originating from the south of France, she moved to the north for her studies, then to Montreal to evolve in a more militant artistic environment. Finally, she settled in Rotterdam where she confronts her Latin-Mediterranean background to the Dutch but mainly multinational cultural scene.

As a politically involved multidisciplinary artist, Aubane Berthommé Martinez uses various mediums (mainly photography and painting) to explore, question, and re-construct elements defining one's identity and power dynamics (gender, sexuality, perceived race, positioning in contemporary capitalism system...). Her visual aesthetics combine pop culture, poetry, kitsch and extravagance.

In 2020 she created Squish, a queer and feminist platform and collective organizing cultural events. Via Squish, she organizes podcasts, exhibitions, workshops, and parties, all celebrating and highlighting the political implications of LGBTQIA+ identities.

As a [wo]man is a research project, resulting from a year of quantitative experiments. As a feminist artist aiming to deconstruct gender roles, I had decided to take distance with the theories that were leading my practice, and focus on gender representations held in the population. A few times per month, I gathered small groups of random strangers (over 100 people in total) in front of my camera and asked them to react to fictional situations by acting. The first few months, the questions asked evolved from a shooting to another, in order to develop a larger panel of reactions and explore a maximum of aspects of my topic (such as gender performance, masculinity and group dynamics, freedom in public space...). Shooting sessions were always followed by a discussion, to let the participants share their experience and see how it impacted them. Most of the time, they were surprized by their own thoughts (for example realizing that binarity of gender/gender expression was a social construction), or realized their male or heterosexual privilege (mainly from the acting of "waiting for the train"/"waiting for the train as a man"/"waiting for the train as a woman"/"waiting for the train as a male gay couple"/"waiting for the train as a female gay couple").

This research helped me develop my practice by understanding body language, gender performances, and how I should interact with my cishet male models as a queer woman. Watching this video again after four years makes me realized how different I am now. I've been through a deconstructing and theorizing process of gender and sexual identities, became more aware and confident, embracing queerness and fluidity of identities.

AS A [WO]MAN

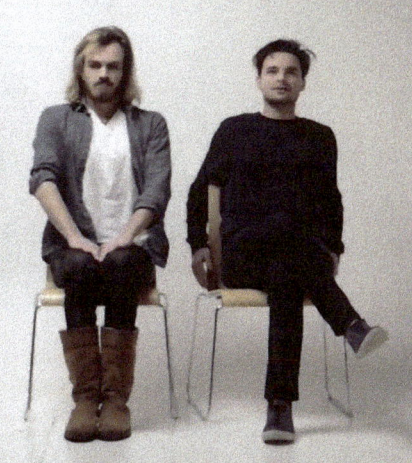

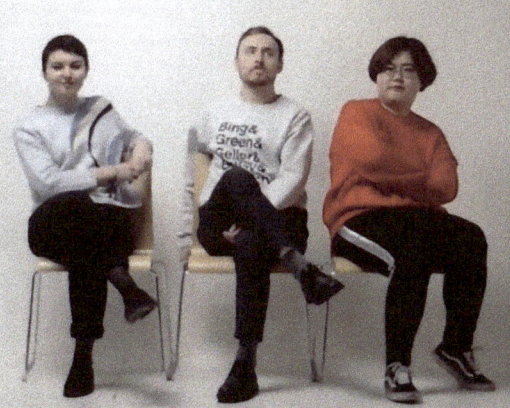

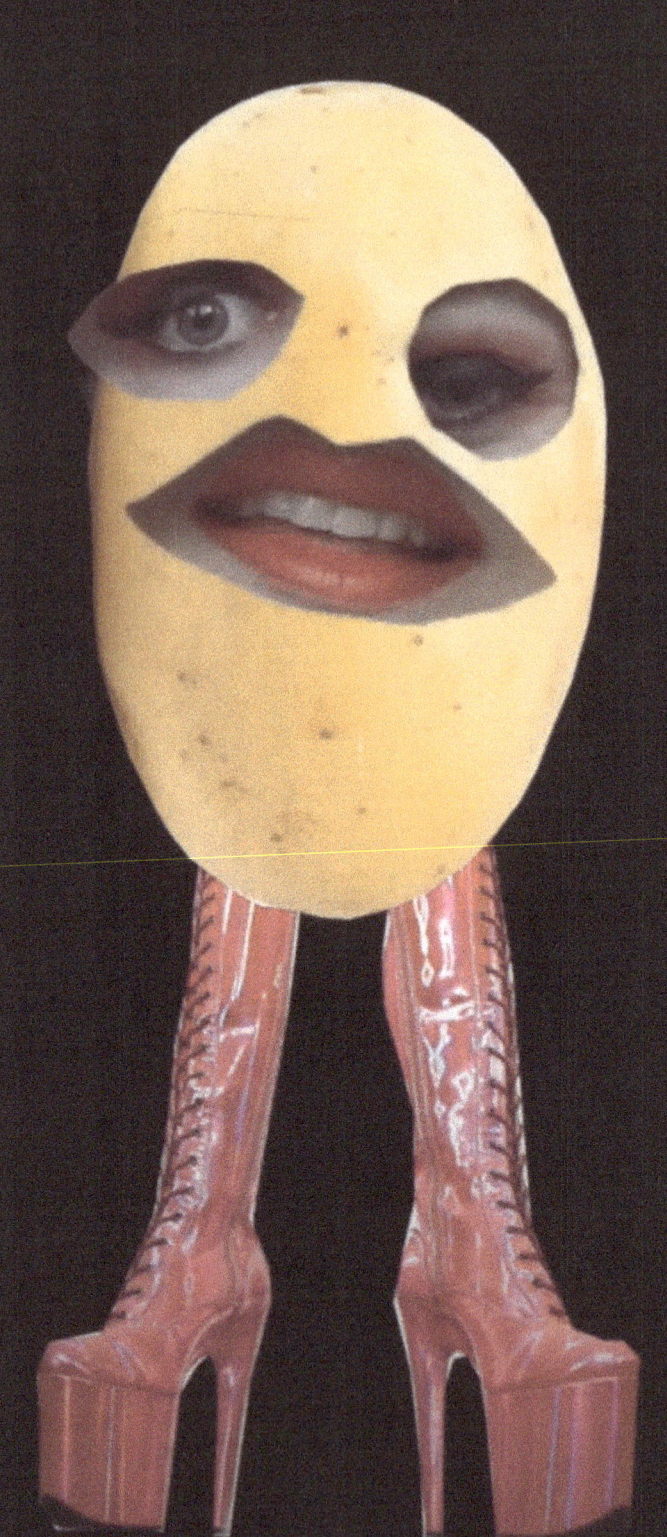

CHARLIE WOOD

Charlie Wood is an artist, performer and writer working in many mediums and forms. Their work explores Queer outrage, contemporary mythology and the intersection of comedy and tragedy. They recently graduated from Central Saint Martins and since then have created work for Les Enfants Terribles, Gash Theatre and Damien Frost. They have performed at The Glory and Royal Vauxhall Tavern and they are an associate artist with Created a Monster Theatre. They have featured in work by John Cameron Mitchell, Gillian Wearing and have recently been commissioned by The Wardrobe

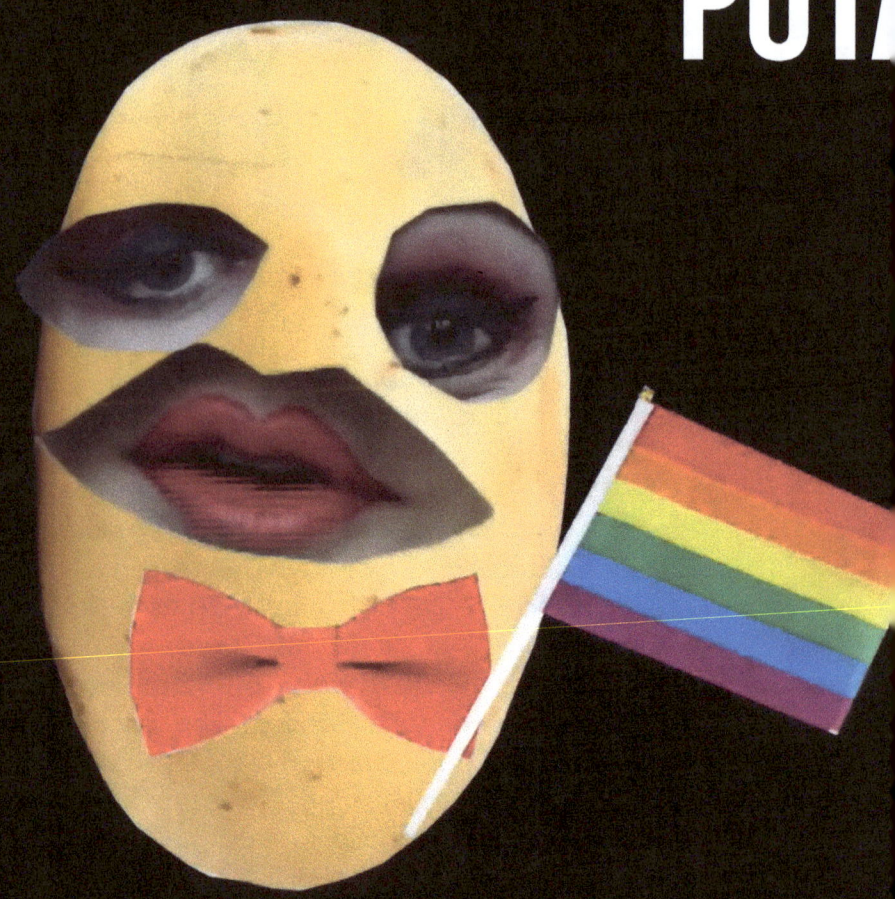

POTA

OES DON'T MATTER

'Potatoes Don't Matter' is a short, illustrated lecture by Charlie Wood responding to the recent controversy surrounding the rebranding of the classic toy 'Mr Potato Head' as the gender neutral 'Potato Head'. Conservatives all over the world cried cancel culture and 'trans activism' but it seems that was always the plan. In the Charlie, using an original video collaging technique explores the issue with high potato fashion, dead pan humour and anti-capitalist politics. The online culture wars are a site of manufactured outrage to distract from the real centres of power and the attention economy is as stacked in favour of the rich as the actual economy. This exists as a problem far beyond Mx Potato head but this was a clear example that the artist used to make comment on the current state of identity, culture, power and the so called 'trans debate'. The video also features a song, performed by Frankie Thompson and dedicated to Piers Morgan.

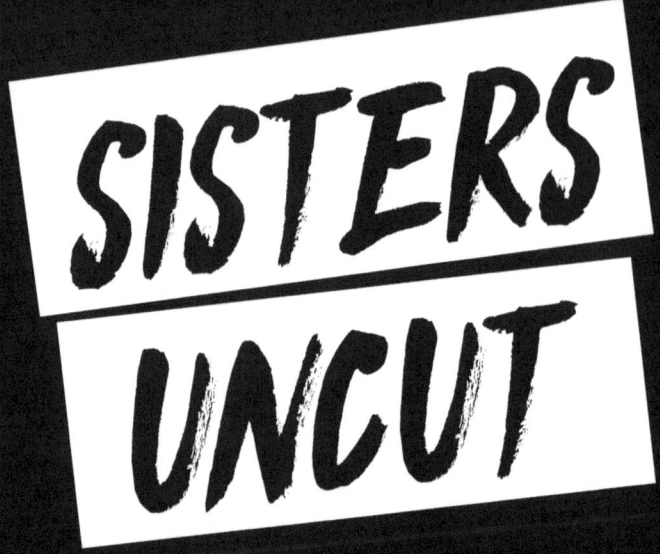

Sisters Uncut collective- an intersectional feminist direct-action collective of of Woman identifying persons and non-binary people. The group main activity is campaigning against domestic abuse, for better domestic violence services, and other related issues. As a collective Sister Uncut has no leaders and no hierarchy. The group decisions are made by a process called consensus decision making, which gives every member of the group an equal say and tries to make sure everyone is happy with the action the group takes. For more information on consensus, see here:

www.sistersuncut.org
www.facebook.com/sistersuncut/

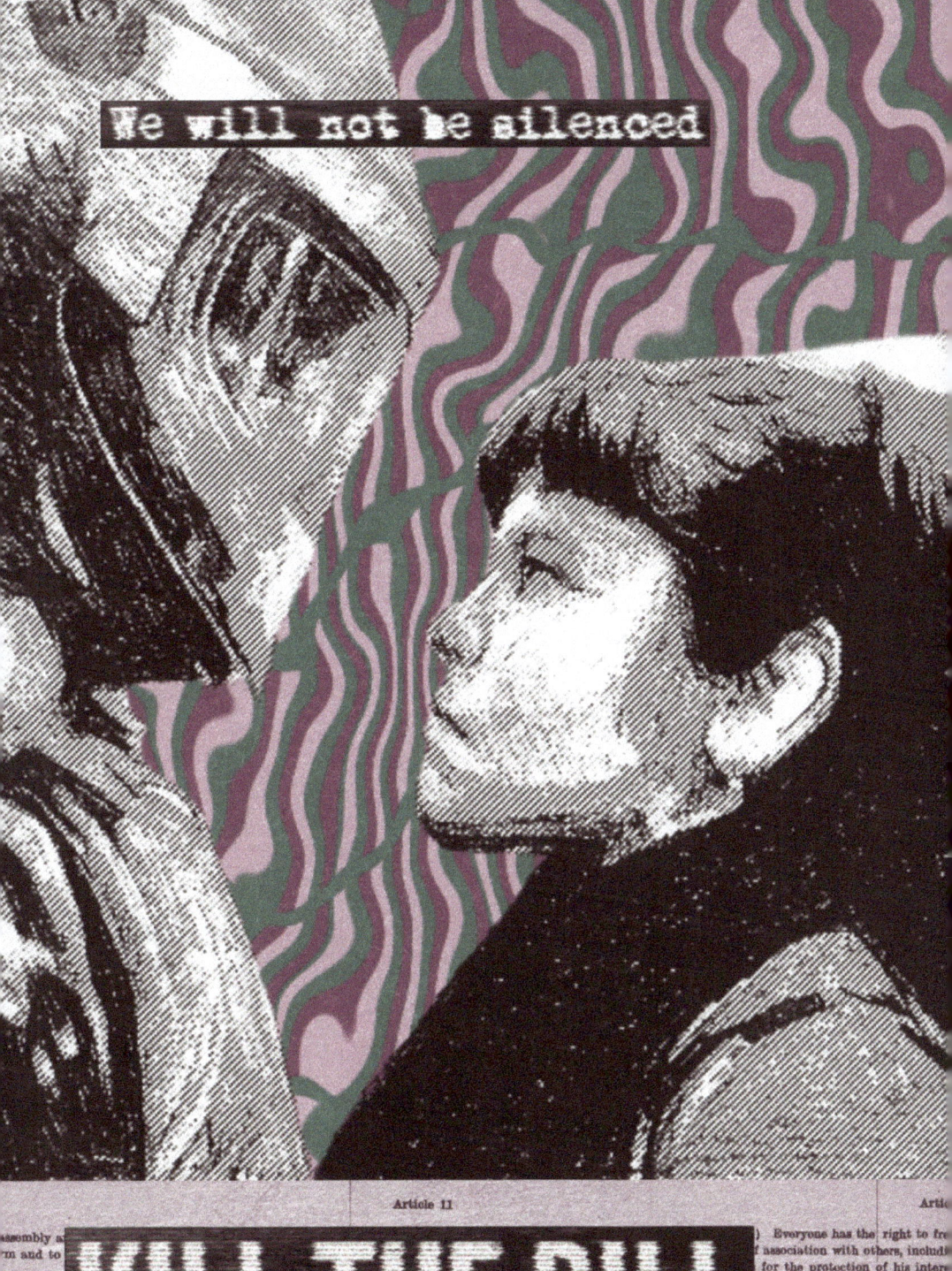

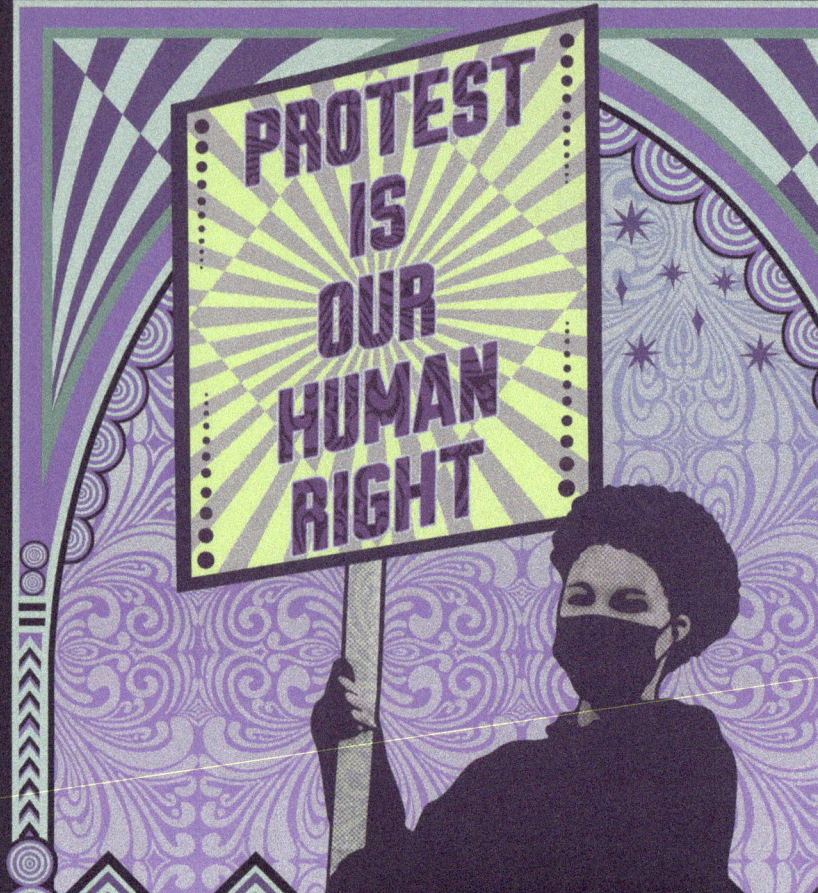

PROTEST IS OUR HUMAN RIGHT

KILL THE BILL

Frank Riot for Sisters Uncut

PROTECT

KILL

GYPSY, ROMA
AND TRAVELLER
COMMUNITIES!
SEX WORKERS!
DISABLED PPL!
TRANS* FOLKS!
BLACK YOUTH!
WORKING CLASS PPL!
RIGHT 2 PROTEST!

#KillTheBill @SistersUncut #KillTheBill @SistersUncut #KillTheBill

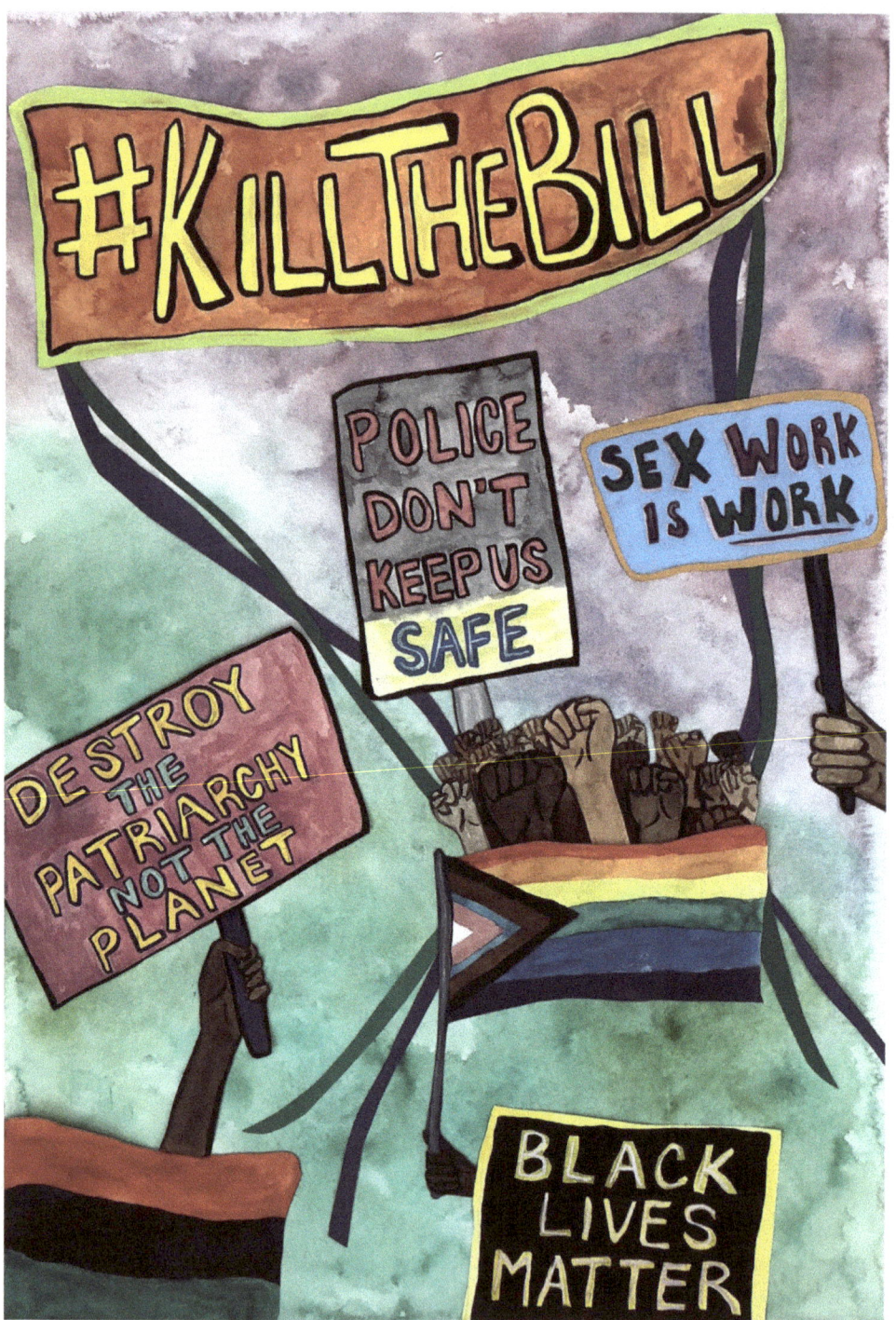

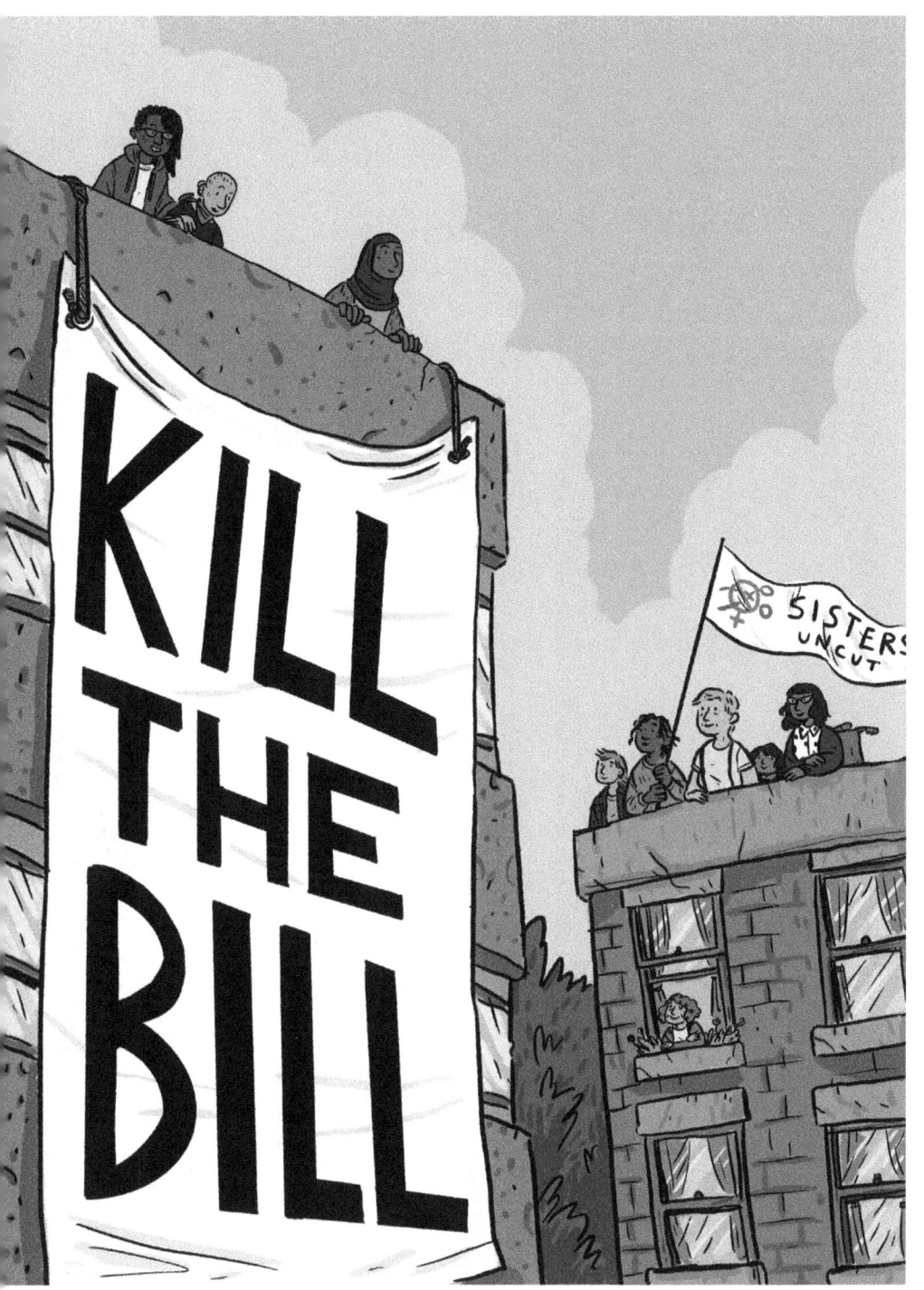

THIS BEING HUMAN IS A GUEST HOUSE.

EVERY MORNING A NEW ARRIVAL.
A JOY, A DEPRESSION, A MEANNESS,
SOME MOMENTARY AWARENESS COMES
AS AN UNEXPECTED VISITOR.
WELCOME AND ENTERTAIN THEM ALL
EVEN IF THEY'RE A CROWD OF SORROWS,
WHO VIOLENTLY SWEEP YOUR HOUSE
EMPTY OF ITS FURNITURE,
STILL, TREAT EACH GUEST HONORABLY.
HE MAY BE CLEARING YOU OUT
FOR SOME NEW DELIGHT.
THE DARK THOUGHT, THE SHAME, THE MALICE,
MEET THEM AT THE DOOR LAUGHING,
AND INVITE THEM IN.
BE GRATEFUL FOR WHOEVER COMES,
BECAUSE EACH HAS BEEN SENT
AS A GUIDE FROM BEYOND.

JALĀL AD-DĪN MOHAMMAD RŪMĪ

Jalāl ad-Dīn Mohammad Rūmī, (30 September 1207 – 17 December 1273), was a 13th-century Persian poet, Hanafi faqih, Islamic scholar, Maturidi theologian, and Sufi mystic originally from Greater Khorasan in Greater Iran. Rumi's influence transcends national borders and ethnic divisions: Iranians, Tajiks, Turks, Greeks, Pashtuns, other Central Asian Muslims, and the Muslims of the Indian subcontinent have greatly appreciated his spiritual legacy for the past seven centuries. His poems have been widely translated into many of the world's languages and transposed into various formats. Rumi has been described as the "most popular poet" and the "best selling poet" in the United States

www.ingramcontent.com/pod-product-compliance
Lightning Source LLC
Chambersburg PA
CBHW041646200526
45172CB00022BA/1282